CRAZY-Wise

The Mindset of a "Peculiar" People

CRAZY-Wise

The Mindset of a "Peculiar" People

Victorious G.E. Blessing

Bladensburg, MD

CRAZYWise

Published by
Inscript Books
a division of Dove Christian Publishers
P.O. Box 611
Bladensburg, MD 20710-0611
www.dovechristianpublishers.com

Copyright © 2020 by Victorious G.E. Blessing

Cover Design by Nadia Chatsworth

ISBN: 978-1-7348625-2-2

All rights reserved. No part of this publication may be used or reproduced without permission of the publisher, except for brief quotes for scholarly use, reviews or articles.

Scriptures quotations, unless otherwise marked, are from the New King James Version®. Copyright © 1982 by Thomas Nelson. Used by permission. All rights reserved.

Published in the United States of America

This book, a product of the divine intervention and inspiration of the Holy Spirit, is dedicated to my family with love

Contents

Preface ix

Chapter 1
Mental Journey to Inner Peace 1

Chapter 2
Liberty and Enlightenment for Life 12

Chapter 3
Heaven Spun Wisdom 22

Chapter 4
Appealing to The Heart of God 36

Chapter 5
The Error of Our Ways 46

Chapter 6
Men of Vision and Purpose 65

Chapter 7
Virtuous Women 75

Chapter 8
"Suffer the Little Children to Come unto Me" 85

Chapter 9
Basking in Jesus 101

Chapter 10
C-R-A-Z-Y–The Acronym 119

Scripture References 122

"I am come that you might have life and have it more abundantly" (John 10:10)

Preface

After years of merely existing as a Christian, frustration built to the point where I realized that there had to be more to life than what I was doing, feeling, and accomplishing. To be "born-again" had to mean more than what was evident in me as well as many of the other professing Christians that I observed or interacted with. What does it mean to be a born-again believer in today's society? What should a true follower of Christ look like in this day and time? Is what I am doing all I was meant to do or accomplish in this life? These questions, along with many others, eventually lead to a very private and earnest spiritual quest for affirmation and clarity.

In the immediate wake of this forty-day quest, it became abundantly clear where and what the anomalies were and what should be done to fix these anomalies. During this spiritual quest, which included fasting, studying the Bible, and praying to Almighty God, I was spiritually assailed with affirmations and instructions that are meant to inspire and motivate Christians to continue the good fight of faith. This rebirth in perspective revealed countless spiritual truths and facts about what is expected of every "born-again" believer regardless of their station in life.

Frankly, it was as if I were overflowing, and I felt deeply compelled to share my journey from a state of mental defeat and oppression to a place of spiritual liberation. Hence, the key message and primary purpose of this book are to make clear the mandate for the true followers of Christ, which is so pure and simple that it is often disregarded or considered optional or downright impractical. The mandate is this: "Seek ye first the kingdom of God, and His righteousness; and all these things shall be added unto you (Matthew 6:33)." This means doing the will of God and being of service to others, sometimes at the expense of personal comforts, trusting that it is all ultimately for our own good. This is indeed a very CRAZY idea to many of us. Yet, those who are wise follow this mandate because they realize that living this way results in an overflow of abundance in all the ways that truly matter.

CHAPTER 1

Mental Journey to Inner Peace

The Journey Begins

My initial journey as a believer began at the age of fourteen. My eldest sister, who had attended a recent revival meeting at a nearby church, had become a Christian or gotten "saved," as they called it. True to kind, she started going to church often, reading her Bible and praying a lot. She even "spoke in tongues." She was different, and in my opinion, she had certainly changed! She adopted some better habits, and she started hanging out with other individuals who also professed to be Christians. I was fascinated by what she was doing, and I wanted to be just like her. Hence, whenever I had free time, I started to spend more time at home instead of going to the neighbor's or hanging out at my friend's house.

It was mid-morning on a Saturday. I had just finished my chores, and everyone else had gone to my grandmother's house to visit. I decided to sit in solitude and just mull over some things that were on my mind. The Christmas season was drawing near, but instead of thinking about presents or decorating, I was thinking about the end of the year and resolutions for the year ahead. Without deliberate intent, I started to talk out loud to God and tell him about my dreams, my hopes, and my desires. I talked about everything and anything that came to my mind. At first, it didn't feel like anything special at all. If anyone had walked into the room, they would have seen me sitting there all alone and would have assumed that I was having the biggest conversation with myself.

Nonetheless, I kept talking, and suddenly, I was overwhelmed with feelings of love, warmth, and gratitude, because I felt as if I was being embraced by God Himself. For the first time, I felt accepted, truly understood, and genuinely loved, without having to be politically correct or sophisticated. I had found a positive outlet and the greatest of all confidants. The One who didn't think I was weird or crazy, and The One who didn't try to talk me into downsizing my dreams to match my reality. The next step was so natural and so sincere; I don't think that I could ever duplicate it again. I asked God to forgive me for all my sins, and I asked Jesus to come into my heart. This made me feel extra good inside. As a matter of fact, I felt as if I could do anything. I was at peace with the world, and I felt as though I could genuinely love everyone. I truly believe that God was in that room with me, and I know that Jesus came into my heart that day. Since that time, I have been physically baptized or immersed in water twice. I was baptized at the age of fifteen because I was told I had to do so as a symbol of my faith. However, when I got baptized again years later as a mature believer, it was a conscious decision to signify the change in the season of my life as it relates to my faith walk and my renewed commitment to being a follower of Christ.

Reflections

The relationship I had with God and my Savior Jesus Christ during my early years as a Christian is a far cry from the relationship that I have with my Creator and my Savior today. During those years, I got to know God through the preachers or pastors of the churches that I attended or from watching and listening to the professing Christians in my immediate surroundings and the wider community. The truth is, I was not brought up in a Christian home. I was not taken to Sunday school, and I was not taught any biblical principles as a strict or specific way of living. However, I do recall that my mother was always admonishing my siblings and me with phrases like, "manners takes you through the world," "cleanliness is next to godliness," and "have respect for your elders." Furthermore, cheating, stealing, lying, and disobedience were never tolerated and always led to a spanking or some other form of punishment. In retrospect, I realize that my mother, even though not a Christian, was reinforcing some watered-down biblical principles for living that had been handed down through generations of individuals who had heard about or believed but had never sought God for themselves.

Even though my mother did her best to instill some values that would cause her children to grow up to be decent citizens, it was all a toss-up, because at the end of the day, no matter how 'normal' or 'good' we may or may not have turned out, we all needed a Savior. Many people do not like to talk about the things they do not understand, and they most certainly do not want to talk about what happens after a person dies. As an enlightened believer, however, I now know that a person can live all of his or her life in denial of the existence of the Almighty God, but there is absolutely no human being who can guarantee that death is the end of all things or that the 'soul' of a person has a finite expiration date. Therefore, when an individual acknowledges the fact that there is life after death and that Almighty God is the judge who has ultimate control over what happens to the never-dying soul of a person, even a fool would realize that he needs a Savior.

Almighty God, in His amazing redemption plan for His creation, has orchestrated the great escape from eternal damnation for all humankind, by sending His only begotten Son to die for the sins of the world. As human beings, we believe we understand and know enough to question or criticize the character of Almighty God, who is so full of love and beauty; yet, He has created a place so utterly horrible and indescribable as Hell. First, our human minds cannot even begin to fathom and understand the ways of Almighty God. He is perfect and does all things well! Second, Hell was not created for humankind! Hell was specially designed as the ultimate, truly horrifying, and eternal punishment for Satan and other fallen angels or unclean spirits—the ones who have been wreaking havoc on humankind and the world for ages.

Finally, Jesus said that He went to prepare a place for those who believe in Him (John 14:3); so, whether that be the new heaven or the new earth (Revelation 21:1-7), the promise is that Christ's followers will spend eternity in His presence. Unfortunately, anyone who rejects Jesus as Lord and Savior has chosen to make Hell their destiny for eternity (Revelation 21: 8). Hell is a spiritual place of unfathomable torment and eternal separation from God. If we choose to live lives that lead us to this place, we cannot blame God. How can you rightly accuse someone of causing you to get wet or catch a cold in the rain after you were provided with an umbrella, a raincoat, a hat, and boots to use for your protection and you did not use them?

Muddling Through and Mucking Along

Over the years, I have gotten 'drenched' quite a few times, and I have certainly had my share of proverbial colds, all because I chose not to use what was given to me to use for my own protection or because I misused what was given to me for my own benefit. In those moments, I was always looking for someone or something to blame for the heartache or hardships that were ultimately self-inflicted.

It is very critical to note that ever since I became a Christian at the age of fourteen, my life has been a series of trial-and-error situations and quite a few questionable decisions. There were periods of days, months, and even a few years where my actions were very uncharacteristic of a true Christian. However, even though I did not fully understand what I was professing or what it meant to be a true Christian at the time, I know for sure that Almighty God Himself had and has saved me! I shudder to think what my life may have been or would be like today if God had not intervened when He did. Despite being a defeated Christian, living an unnecessary extended season as a victim, God never left me! All along, I was the one not paying attention to His boundless forgiveness and His amazing love for me. Therefore, I give God, the Holy Spirit, and my Savior Jesus Christ all the credit for every wonderful opportunity I have had and for every good, useful, and selfless thing that I have ever done. I also give God thanks for turning around all the things that were meant to destroy me and for creating beauty out of the ashes that could have been my life.

Fourteen was an age where I was still too young to grasp a full understanding of the magnitude of who God is and what believing in Him meant for me. However, I was old enough to realize that my life without Christ would be a total waste and that I was headed to a place called Hell if I did not accept the Lord Jesus as my personal Savior and try to live for Him the best I could for the rest of my life. My past experiences have taught me that living for Christ is much easier said than done. However, the Holy Spirit has helped me to certainly realize that living for Christ is a reality that must be practiced and only gets better when we make a deliberate effort to live by faith. It is also imperative to realize that if or when we do not use the "gift of Jesus" as prescribed, we do so at the risk of damning our very souls.

As I alluded to earlier, the God and the Jesus that I got to know during my early years are certainly not the God and the Jesus that I know today. In retrospect, I must admit that during my early years as a Christian, I was in definite training to become a first-rate scribe or Pharisee. Jesus Himself would not have recognized me as a follower. It was as if I had forgotten that God had shown me mercy and rescued me from a definite path of self-destruction. I was an ignorant, hypocritical, judgmental and self-serving fool in so many ways, for far too long.

In John 10:27, Jesus states, "My sheep hear My voice, and I know them and they follow Me." As an immature believer, I had assumed that this was an automatic reality since being a Christian meant "follower of or believer in Christ." I had yet to realize that recognizing and following God's voice was not a "one-time" event but necessitates a deliberate relationship with the Holy Spirit, which would lead to a state of mind that would make me more susceptible to the voice and the call of God. It finally dawned on me that if a Christian does not make a conscious effort to immerse him or herself in God's word and spend time seeking God, the voice of God will continue to go unheeded in that individual's life. Therefore, that Christian would find him or herself being more in tune with humankind's wisdom and traditions rather than the life-transforming power that comes from *really* hearing and following God's voice. The impact of this realization was like scales falling away from my eyes to make visible all the truths that were already in plain sight.

Restless

During my early years as a Christian, I had become increasingly aware that there was more to me and my life than what I was doing and experiencing, but I seemed unable to tap into the Higher Power that would get me out of the rut that I was stuck in. Nonetheless, I thought that since I believed in Jesus and accepted Him into my heart as my Lord and Savior and tried my best to do what was right from that point onward, this meant that I had heard God's voice and was doing His will. However, the truth is, I was spiritually hard of hearing. Fortunately, God's voice began to infiltrate this impenetrable wall of oppression one fateful Sunday while I sat in church. Ever since then, I have begun to fully appreciate my place and purpose in this world as a follower of Christ.

Here's what happened. I was dutifully listening to the sermon when the following words suddenly invaded my thoughts: "the Spirit of the Lord is upon me because He has anointed me for such a time as this." These words were so audible that it took a minute for me to realize that the pastor had not said them and that the sermon was not directly related to what I had just heard. Apparently, my mind had strayed. I had started to think about what I could and should be doing as a Christian in a society that seemed so determined to destroy itself. However, in my "lukewarm" or oppressed state, I was unable to appreciate the significance and the direct connection between these words and my thoughts. Instead, I became preoccupied and more concerned about where I had heard or read similar words before.

I felt compelled to locate this text in my Bible, and before the service ended that day, I had found the passage that I was looking for in the gospel of Luke. "The Spirit of the Lord is upon Me, because He has anointed Me to preach the gospel to the poor; He has sent Me to heal the brokenhearted, to proclaim liberty to the captives, and the recovery of sight to the blind; to set at liberty those who are oppressed; to proclaim the acceptable year of the Lord" (Luke 4:18-19). I realized that Isaiah had prophesied these words about my Lord and Savior and that at the beginning of His ministry, Jesus declared that this prophecy was fulfilled in Him.

Locating the Scripture did not satisfy me as I thought it would. Instead, I began to feel haunted because I kept hearing the words that Jesus spoke at the beginning of His ministry, and I could not help feeling that these words meant something special and specific to me. At first, I prayed and asked for forgiveness because I thought that I was being blasphemous or presumptuous for identifying with a Scripture that was directly fulfilled in Jesus Christ. Nevertheless, the words kept invading my thoughts, and I became so frustrated about the conflict in my mind that I started to cry at one point. In my lukewarm and ignorant state, I sincerely did not know what I was supposed to do with a Scripture that was already fulfilled in the Lord Jesus Christ.

I read Isaiah 61 and Luke 4 repeatedly, trying to get a better understanding of what these words meant to me. I understood that these words epitomized Jesus' ministry on Earth, but as I mentioned, I was so spiritually deaf and blind that it took a while for me to realize that Jesus' entire and exact ministry was now the responsibility of His true followers. I did not permit myself to share what I was going through with any other human being because I am often predisposed not to trust or be satisfied with the advice or the well-intentioned explanations of other people. Therefore, I kept praying to God to help me and reveal to me exactly how I was supposed to respond or react to these words.

Finally, I felt led to embark on a spiritual quest where I fasted for a time, prayed constantly, and studied the scriptures intensely, fervently seeking answers and peace of mind for the inner turmoil that I was experiencing. This forty-day quest took place a few months after my thirty-first birthday. No other person knew what I was going through during the months prior or what I was really up to during these forty days. I can say without any doubt that the Holy Spirit helped me to keep it together and remain highly productive in every area of my life throughout the entire experience. Furthermore, my earnest quest for answers resulted in a spiritual transformation and state of enlightenment so phenomenal that I felt as though I had been awakened from a deep, long, and dark stupor.

Forgetting to Rest in Jesus

Before my spiritual awakening, I was a constant victim of religious affliction and condemnation either from myself or from the "well-meaning" Christians around me. I felt as though I had to be perfect in every way if I professed to be a Christian. I believed that since I "claimed" to have accepted Jesus Christ as my Lord and Savior, I had to spend the rest of my life tiptoeing around as if "walking on eggshells." The harder I tried to be perfect, the more mistakes I made and the louder the voice of accusation taunted my conscience. I believed that when I fell short of certain religious standards or made a mistake, I was not a good Christian and something was wrong with me. Maybe I was not even "saved" or a Christian at all. I compared myself to those individuals who seemed to have it all together or seemed to be having such good success with their Christian walk because it appeared as though they never lost their tempers or got caught up in the lusts of the flesh.

For years, I had failed miserably at being a "good Christian," and I continued to fail in many areas, no matter how I proposed to do better over and over again. Some might ask, why try to be something that caused so much inner turmoil and made me feel so bad about myself when there were people who would accept me for who I was, just as I was? Well, the truth is, when I accepted Jesus as my Lord and Savior at the age of fourteen, I made a vow to serve Him for the rest of my life. It was a sincere, heartfelt promise, and my conscience kept reminding me of it. Furthermore, I continued to crave decency and order as well as right standing with my Heavenly Father despite my contrary actions. However, due to misguided teachings and beliefs, I was unable to keep my promise or live up to God's standards, simply because I kept trying to do it all under my own strength. I had never grasped hold of the revelation knowledge that my righteousness and my ability to walk victoriously as a Christian required me to look to Jesus, trust in Jesus, hide in Jesus and depend on Jesus in all things for the rest of my life. However, the good news is that God had heard the sincere promise that I had made all those years ago, and He had been continually working behind the scenes to bring me to the point where I would eventually realize the gift and the purpose that was lying dormant within me all this time.

Imagine the inner turmoil of an individual who claimed to have accepted the gift of salvation at the age of fourteen and, many years later, was still having difficulty with the laws and standards of Christian living. I believed that after all this time, I should have been "perfect," or at least I should have mastered the basic principles of Christian living. Unfortunately, I was still a religious mess, condemned by the impossible standards that I had set for myself or had allowed others to impose upon me. The harder I tried to live a perfect life, the more I messed up and the more mistakes I made. There were occasions when I was so far off course that I was too embarrassed to tell anyone that I was a Christian. After all, how could I be a Christian when my life was so riddled with mistakes and shortcomings to the point that I thought I was an embarrassment to God Himself? There were times when I made mistakes and just wallowed in them. Instead of trusting in God to help me out of my predicament, I stayed down and was the victim of my own condemnation for so long that I almost convinced myself that I could do no better, so I might as well just go with the flow. Like I said, "inner turmoil." This means that from the outside looking in, everything was normal or going as well as it could be expected. However, I was constantly fighting for my life on the battlefield of my mind.

Throughout my years of falling and struggling to get back up again, God was merciful to me. He never gave up on me. His hands were always extended out toward me. So, when I finally reached up from my downtrodden state in an attempt to grasp at that lifeline, God Himself pulled me up and drew me into a closer walk with Him. It is the recognition of God's unfailing love and unmerited favor that has propelled me into a more victorious and purpose-filled life. The Spirit of God finally made me realize that I was failing and would continue to fail unless I rested in Him. I was not falling short and making mistakes because I was sitting still, being complacent, or not trying at all. I was falling short because I was too busy setting my own standards for Godly living and trying to live up to them under my own strength. For years, I had been living like the Israelites when they were in the desert. The journey to their destination was such a short distance, and yet they spent forty years wandering around in the desert. Similarly, the journey to my spiritual awakening was prolonged simply because I relied heavily on the approval or opinions of other people and trusted in my own strength and abilities far too often, instead of looking to Jesus and trusting in God.

Light at The End of The Tunnel

After becoming aware of my spiritual purpose and the power that is within me because of Jesus Christ, I am now able to stand up without any "crutches" or validation from others. I am no longer Satan's punching bag, doormat, or latest joke. I am now a victorious child of God who knows that if I forget to walk by faith or mistakenly "walk in the flesh," God does not and will not condemn me or cast me aside. Therefore, I no longer need to stay down, be stepped on, or wallow in the mud of my mistakes; instead, I can look to Jesus for forgiveness and deliverance as well as the strength to get up and continue pressing toward the mark of a higher calling in Jesus Christ. Jesus is my Salvation! He died and has already been punished for my sins, so there is no need to allow myself to be punished again and again unnecessarily for a debt that has already been paid in full!

As an ambassador for Christ, the Anointed One, I walk with the power of the Holy Spirit within me. This means that I have the power to resist sin and temptation the same way that Jesus did when He walked on the face of this earth. Unfortunately, if I continue to sin and be a victim of the same shortcomings again, it implies that the Christ (the Spirit of God) within me is no match for the sins and temptations of the world. However, 1 John 4:4 teaches that "greater is He who is within me than he who is in the world." Therefore, I know that I have the power to walk in the Spirit, overcome all things, and not fulfill the lusts of the flesh. As a born-again believer, my eyes have been opened to realize that sin and iniquity can no longer reign in my life or have dominion over me. I am a new creation in Christ, which means that my old sinful ways have been crucified on Calvary, and I can live in victory each day by having my mind renewed continuously with this spiritual reality.

My spiritual awakening has caused me to realize that the gift of salvation is far too precious to squander away by continually making the same foolish mistakes and needlessly living life with a "victim" mentality. I am now acutely aware that with the anointing of the Holy Spirit upon me and within me, it is my duty to carry out the mandate of Jesus Christ. I also understand that, as an ambassador of the kingdom of heaven, I must function under the mantle of Jesus Christ, which is clearly outlined in the book of Isaiah chapter 61 in the passage that declares, "The Spirit of the Lord is upon Me, because He has anointed me to preach the gospel to the poor; He has sent Me to heal the brokenhearted, to proclaim liberty to the captives, and the recovery of sight to the blind; to set at liberty those who are oppressed; to proclaim the acceptable year of the Lord." The revelation that my anointing, my purpose, my life's mission, my victory, and my prosperity are all clearly associated with and dependent upon my acceptance of the amazing gift that is in Jesus Christ has led to indescribable inner peace, exceptional purpose, and a Christ-centric state of mind that is definitely out of this world. As Jesus said in John 14:27, "Peace I leave with you, My peace I give to you; not as the world gives do I give you. Let not your heart be troubled, neither let it be afraid."

CHAPTER 2

Liberty and Enlightenment for Life

Our God is Truly Patient

A divinely orchestrated spiritual awakening is such a life-transforming and liberating experience! Consequently, as ambassadors for the kingdom of heaven, we ought to remember that our God, the amazing Creator, orchestrates the most significant circumstances in whatever form or fashion He deems fit to activate our true purpose in this world. Hence, in Galatians 5:1, believers are admonished to "stand fast therefore in the liberty by which Christ has made you free, and do not be entangled again with the yoke of bondage." I declare that as a direct result of seeking God's face, I began to feel more loved, forgiven, liberated, and validated. The Lord allowed me to understand that the words of Isaiah 61, which He had been hammering into my heart and mind, were simply to activate my mission and purpose as a kingdom ambassador. As a disciple of Jesus Christ, it is my esteemed privilege to walk in His footsteps and my duty to ensure that His message is shared with anyone who is still lost, uncertain, or spiritually oppressed.

Many of you may have been aware of this truth for quite a while now and may or may not have been totally transformed by this knowledge. However, as I mentioned before, prior to this life-transforming revelation, I had always considered myself to be a Christian but never truly understood my purpose and simply went through the motions of trying to satisfy my own self-righteous standards. In my ignorance and lukewarm state, I was not doing a good job of representing or sharing Jesus Christ. Furthermore, I hardly ever went out of my way to display a Christ-like disposition in my relationships or interactions with others.

Fortunately, God is extremely patient and merciful. So, during my journey to spiritual enlightenment, the Holy Spirit taught me well and allowed me to understand that Jesus is the answer to all things and that the scriptures are fulfilled in Him. Jesus came to Earth and did what no one else had done or could ever do. He did what no other priest, prophet, king, patriarch, or leader did before or after Him. A review of the lives and exploits of every other prophet, patriarch, king, priest, or leader mentioned in the Bible, or anywhere else, will reveal shortcomings that were never found in Jesus Christ. Jesus was truly original and the trailblazer of a ministry like no other. His ministry and life on Earth literally encompassed the things that were prophesied about Him. He went about healing the sick, feeding the hungry, reassuring and providing hope for the outcasts, educating the masses, and extending mercy without partiality. He spoke up for the poor and the oppressed, and He preached against the self-righteous or damning tendencies of humankind. He then became a willing sacrifice so that He could make the amazing gift of salvation and the cloak of His righteousness available to every human being who believes in Him.

The Holy Spirit is The Best Teacher

Jesus died for the salvation of humankind so that all of God's children could experience abundant lives now and everlasting life in the world to come. The Holy Spirit allowed me to finally digest and benefit from spiritual truths, such as the fact that it is not God's will that anyone should perish, but that we all may have eternal life (2 Peter 3:9). My spiritual eyes were opened to receive that when we accept Jesus as our Lord and Savior, He comes and dwells within us and causes our spirit to awaken so that the image of God can shine through us. As Christians, when we become enlightened, it is our duty to proclaim and live the good news of the gospel every day and share this treasure with anyone who is still in darkness. We should strive to continually walk by faith and unwavering belief in the power of God, constantly shaking off the image in 2

Timothy 3: 1-5, where men are described as selfish, coldhearted, haughty, greedy, and as "having a form of godliness but denying its power." I believe that a major problem with Christianity today is that there are many individuals who attempt to share the good news of the gospel when they are still living in spiritual oppression. It is hypocritical to sell a product that you have never personally experienced or used because you won't do a good job representing the product or convincing others to try it for themselves.

Before my spiritual awakening, I was not liberated enough to be of any real benefit to the advancement of the kingdom of heaven on this earth. I was a useless Christian, living in spiritual poverty; my light was out, I had no flavor, and my "talent" was buried in the ground. I was accustomed to "keeping it together" and appearing right in the eyes of my peers, but I had never truly introspected and considered my life through the eyes of the Holy Spirit. My lukewarm state as a Christian reminded me of the words Jesus spoke in Matthew 15: 8-9: "These people draw near to me with their mouth and honor me with their lips, but their heart is far from Me, teaching as doctrines the commandments of men." The Holy Spirit reminded me that God searches the heart and knows the thoughts of every person. So, no matter how many accolades I may have received for doing what I thought was pleasing in God's sight, I was missing the mark entirely. I was too judgmental, self-righteous, and self-serving. I also lacked true compassion and real empathy toward anyone who was not in my immediate circle of family and friends. Through careful and deliberate introspection, I became acutely aware that I was blatantly immature as a believer. I realized that I needed to apply deliberate effort and spend more quality time in the presence of God so that I could get to know the real Jesus and have His character shine through me.

Love is Liberating

Prior to these revelations, I spent my days trying hard not to commit the "obvious" or "scandalous" sins. Meanwhile, impatience, presumption, selfishness, a sharp tongue, and an unforgiving heart were a part of my daily existence. These are some of the routine sins that we tend to let slide, but when God searches the heart, these are the kinds of things that displease Him and ultimately classify us as lawless. When Christ enters our hearts, the fruit of the Spirit should be allowed to flourish and choke out the weeds of routine sin. However, we must deliberately cultivate good habits and practice the fruit of the Spirit so that we can continue to have dominion over our sinful nature and desires. By Biblical standards, a lawless person is any individual who goes against or disregards a direct command. As true believers, it is our duty to "fear God, and keep His commandments" (Ecclesiastes 12:13). In Matthew 19:17, Jesus says, "But if you want to enter life, keep the commandments." Can you imagine what the world would be like if every Christian was sold-out to Jesus, committed and busy striving daily to love God and others as we were commanded?

In John 15:12, Jesus said, "This is My commandment, that you love one another as I have loved you." Truth be told, there are some distinct qualities about the love that Jesus had for humankind. He never condoned any wrongdoing, and He never condemned the lost, but He loved people out of their sins and into a newness of life. We, as His followers, are called to do the same in our relationships with others. Instead of living in judgment of others, we need to lead with love!

Consequently, I agree with Paul when he told the early church in 1 Corinthians 13 that love is the greatest of all the gifts of the Holy Spirit. This means that without true love, every other gift is of no real benefit to humankind or to the advancement of the kingdom of heaven in this world. Therefore, we should pray for the gift of love and learn to love God and our neighbors as Jesus commanded; then our words, thoughts, and deeds would be more pleasing to Him. Obeying Jesus' direct command removes us from the realm of condemnation and lawlessness and guarantees eternal life.

Empowered for Purpose

As a child of God, it is very exciting and liberating to know that God has placed His Holy Spirit in us to enable us to continue the life-transforming work that Jesus began more than two thousand years ago. In John 14:12, Jesus said, "Most assuredly, I say unto you, he who believes in Me, the works I do he will do also; and greater works than these he will do because I go to My Father." In John 14:26, Jesus further stated that "the Helper, the Holy Spirit, whom the Father will send in My name, He will teach you all things that I said to you." Jesus knew that we can do nothing that truly pleases Him "in and of ourselves." So, He sent the Holy Spirit to dwell within us to enable us to walk in His footsteps. He also knew that our mandate to continue the work that He started would be difficult and sometimes impossible without divine help. Therefore, He did not leave us defenseless. As Christians, we must allow the Holy Spirit to have dominion in our lives so that we would not become immobilized by fear or selfish indulgence and lose sight of our purpose as ambassadors of the kingdom of heaven.

Essentially, the good news of the gospel encompasses humanity's salvation and restoration, which was supremely orchestrated through the birth, life, death, burial, resurrection, and ascension of Jesus Christ. Amazingly, the good news of the gospel is simplified and summarized in one Scripture: "For God so loved the world that He gave His only begotten Son that whosoever believes in Him should not perish but have everlasting life" (John 3:16). This Scripture is so widespread and so familiar that people quote it without realizing the magnitude of it. Nonetheless, the Bible bears repeated witness of God's love for humankind and the awesome orchestration of salvation's plan, which results in manifold blessings in this world and the hope of eternal life in the world to come.

As true Christians, many of us are finding real satisfaction in doing the things that Jesus did when He walked on this earth. True believers have a right to experience healthy, happy, prosperous, and purpose-filled lives on this earth because this is what Jesus meant in John 10:10 when He said, "I have come that they might have life and that they may have it more abundantly." Therefore, as ambassadors of Christ, when we experience hardships and persecutions (which are symptoms and side effects of living in a world where Satan's mission is to kill, steal and destroy every good thing), we should not lose sight of our purpose or forget the power of Christ within us. From an enlightened perspective, our trials should help us to feel a great sense of honor when we think of Hebrews 12: 5-6, which speaks to the fact that God chastens those whom He loves. Moreover, we can also be encouraged by the story of Job (42:10), who lost everything but in the end, he was blessed twice over because he kept the faith and continued to trust in God. So, no matter what, keep the faith and stay true to God.

Jesus Makes the Difference

As believers, it is important to remember that the heart and love of God are far more superior and purer than the heart of any human. As a matter of fact, Godly love is the only kind of love that will enable a Christian to love other people (especially enemies) with the kind of love that Jesus had for us. Godly love is also the anointing that enables a Christian to identify with the life and ministry of Jesus Christ. Unfortunately, Godly love is impossible for our human hearts to emulate, so we must walk steadfastly in the Spirit and draw from the heart of God. In other words, we should continually draw from the resources of the kingdom of God within us. Our love walk is much like Peter walking on water (Matthew 14: 22-33). Once we keep our eyes fastened on Jesus Christ, all things are possible, and we can do anything. Unfortunately, if we take our eyes off Jesus or experience a wave of doubt, if only for the shortest time, we risk sinking into the sea of fear, selfishness, and despair. As children of God, we have been freed from the oppression of sin and released from the captivity of ignorance. We therefore must help our neighbors experience this same kind of freedom. It is also important to realize that this divine liberation is possible only when we embrace who we are "in and through" Jesus Christ. Jesus' sacrifice enables us to be reinstated and victorious members in the family of God.

In Mark 3:35, Jesus states that "whoever does the will of God is My brother and My sister and mother." This means that when we accept the gift of salvation freely given to us by our heavenly Father and allow His will to prevail in our lives, we automatically become members of the family of God. In the Old Testament,

Isaiah prophesied that Jesus was sent to Earth not only to raise up the house of Jacob and restore the preserved ones of Israel but also as a light to the Gentiles and as a vessel of God's salvation for all man (Isaiah 49:6). In the New Testament, Paul affirms, "therefore let it be known to you that the salvation of God has been sent to the Gentiles and they will hear it" (Acts 28: 28). It is as a direct result of Jesus' amazing sacrifice that I can boldly declare that I have been redeemed, and I am indeed a child of the Living God.

Walking fully in the liberty that is afforded us through the sacrifice of our Lord and Savior Jesus Christ necessitates accepting the gift of salvation by faith. In Acts 26:18, God told Paul that He would deliver him from the Gentiles to whom he was sent to preach; "to open their eyes in order to turn them from darkness to light, and from the power of Satan to God, that they may receive forgiveness of sins and an inheritance among those who are sanctified by faith in Me." This means that Jesus made it possible for every sinner (including those outside the bloodline of Jacob or Israelite heritage) to become full-fledged heirs to the promises of God. Therefore, there is absolutely no human being who is excluded or left out of salvation's plan, and Christ's death made it possible for us to be restored as children of God. Paul is the original messenger of grace to the Gentiles, and his experiences and dynamic ministry serve as prime examples of God's ability to forgive, fully transform, and use even "the chief of sinners."

Our Victory is In Jesus

So, what do you do when you fall short as a believer? You simply get up, brush yourself off, ask for forgiveness, and continue moving forward with a repentant heart and with renewed fervor. Be aware that once you accept Jesus as your Lord and Savior and purpose in your heart that you will follow Him, Satan becomes obsessed with trying to make you "fall." Satan's goal is to have you relapse permanently into your old sinful ways so that you can be a failure in the eyes of your peers and also lose out on your opportunity for eternal life. However, falling short is only a small fraction of actual failure. True failure comes when we stay down, continue to fall short in the same areas, accept defeat, and allow ourselves to be trampled on by the enemy. Therefore, when we fall short, we need to be mindful that Jesus Christ has already made us victorious. By acknowledging this fact, we should quickly pick ourselves up, and we should be careful not to get knocked down again without putting up a fight. The aim of every believer who falls should be to get back up again (even when wounded) and cast condemnation aside, because Jesus Christ, who has redeemed you, is waiting to help you win the good fight of faith.

In 1 Peter 2:9-10, the writer affirms, "But you are a chosen generation, a royal priesthood, a holy nation, His own special people, that you may proclaim the praises of Him who called you out of darkness into His marvelous light; who once were not a people but are now the people of God, who had not obtained mercy but now have obtained mercy." As an ambassador for Christ, I find this to be one of the most powerful scriptures of liberation because it helps me to grasp the magnitude of what Jesus' matchless sacrifice accomplished on my behalf and on behalf of every sinner who accepts Him as Lord and Savior.

Crazy or Enlightened?

My Spiritual awakening has been so liberating and intoxicating that some may consider my beliefs and ideas a bit farfetched or overly simplistic. Most people, especially Christians, cringe at the thought of being regarded as crazy, and this is one of the main reasons why there are so many lukewarm and ineffective Christians in the world today. We are more concerned about the approval and wisdom of the "intellectuals" than we are about the anointing and power of God. However, if someone were to call me crazy today because I believe in the awesome gift and opportunity that is in Jesus, I would simply smile. After all, it does seem illogical to place one's faith, hopes, dreams, and future in the power and promises of the unseen God. Nonetheless, I wholeheartedly believe in Almighty God, the Creator of Heaven and Earth and the Sustainer of the universe, as well as the gift of salvation and eternal life which is in Christ Jesus.

I am very aware of the presence of darkness which is perpetuated by Satan and his army of evil spirits all over the world. I believe that Satan is the only true enemy of humankind, and he does not want anything good to happen for us. I am also aware that Satan has been working his plan of deception and hatred to kill, steal, and destroy everything that God, our Creator and Heavenly Father, meant for us to have. However, I am eternally grateful for the precious and powerful blood of Jesus Christ, which makes born-again believers more than conquerors, and the Spirit of God which renders Satan powerless over us or against us. I firmly believe that God is love and that all good things come from Him. I also believe that while we were yet sinners, Christ died for us (Romans 5:8) so that we could live abundantly now and have everlasting life in the world to come.

If by rejecting man's wisdom, logic, and explanations in favor of a wholehearted belief in the Bible and the Most High God means that I am crazy, then so be it. However, I must say that embracing Jesus Christ as my Savior and trusting in God's promises have led to a spiritual liberation that I will not allow anyone to take away from me. As far as being called crazy, I certainly would not be the first believer to have faith in God and reap amazing benefits. After all, patriarchs like Noah, Abraham, Moses, and Daniel are just a few who made some choices and did some things that seemed illogical in the normal system of things. Noah prepared for a major flood, even though there was no physical evidence of even the slightest bit of rain (Genesis 6). Abram left his home and familiar territory to go to a place that he had never seen and of which he had no tangible guarantee (Genesis 12). Moses left the king's palace and the lap of luxury to identify with a people who were still in bondage at the time (Exodus 2). Daniel defied a king's order and continued to pray to Almighty God despite the threat and consequence of the death penalty (Daniel 6). These are just a few examples of people who chose to trust God in extenuating circumstances and could, therefore, be considered crazy. However, I am encouraged because God Himself vindicated and validated these men because of their faith and unfailing belief. Consequently, I believe and accept that the secret to true enlightenment for the abundant and purpose-filled life in Jesus Christ is encompassed in Proverbs 3:5-6, which says, "Trust in the Lord with all your heart and lean not on your own understanding. In all your ways acknowledge Him and He will direct your paths."

For more Scriptural study related to this chapter, go to page 122.

CHAPTER 3

Heaven Spun Wisdom

Whom God Keeps is Well Kept

"Come unto Me, all you who labor and are heavy laden, and I will give you rest" are words of light and life spoken by our Savior in Matthew 11:28. As I alluded to earlier, Jesus is the answer to all things! When we surrender our hearts and will to Him, we begin to experience rest or a heightened sense of peace from the spiritual, emotional, psychological, and physical havoc of this world, on a level that is not of this world. As a spiritually awakened believer, all my hopes, dreams, and aspirations in life are wrapped up in the power, wisdom, love, and authority of Almighty God. I have peace knowing that God is still on His throne, and I am certain that He has my best interest at heart. When I consider who God is and what His plan for humankind was since the beginning of time, I am truly grateful. When I reflect on the incredible way that salvation's plan was laid out in the Bible, I am amazed at the infinite goodness, faithfulness, and love of God toward all people. It is of the utmost importance to note that even though humankind has done everything possible to merit total annihilation, God still extends His forgiveness, mercy, and grace toward us.

Trust the Creator of Heaven and Earth

As human beings in need of a Savior, we continue to err in so many ways. We trust in mere "men," even though humankind is limited and uncertain about so many things. We have not considered that the ways of humanity, as well as our interference with the natural order of things, have caused us to experience many ills and setbacks in this world, such as wars, famines, diseases, and even natural disasters. Despite everything, humankind has been and is still trying to live without God, even in the face of constant reliance on the resources of The Creator. The so-called "intelligent human" can create absolutely nothing unless he has something to begin with, and though he tries, he is limited and has no ultimate control over anything. In Ecclesiastes 1, Solomon wisely concludes that all of man's toils and efforts are vanity. Since "man" can do nothing in and of himself, it makes sense to acknowledge the Supreme power of God and live a life of purpose and abundance in Him. Furthermore, may we remain ever mindful of Proverbs 9:10, which states that "The fear of the Lord is the beginning of wisdom, and the knowledge of the Holy one is understanding."

In Genesis 1, the Bible tells us about our Heavenly Father, the All-Powerful God who created the heavens and the earth from nothing. It also teaches us that God made humankind to rule and have dominion over the things on the earth. However, "man's" fall from grace has subjected humankind to hardships and misappropriation of authority in this world. Instead of repentance for this colossal mistake, the Old Testament gives us detailed accounts of humankind's continued, willful disregard and disobedience of God. Despite God's patience, mercy, favor, and divine intervention, humankind has rebelled against God. Nonetheless, the Bible gives specific commands and statutes to obey so that we can experience abundant and purpose-filled lives on Earth. It also outlines salvation's plan and the reinstatement of humankind back into the family of God. A belief in the accounts and promises recorded in the Bible requires faith. I choose to believe that the Bible is God's word and a road map back to Him. So, the worst that could happen, if the Bible is "just another book," as so many people claim to believe, is that I would have spent my life living with consideration for others and endeavoring to love my neighbor. However, the best thing that could happen if the Bible is indeed the word of God is that I would experience abundant life now with the real hope for eternal life in the world to come. Ultimately, my belief in the Bible as God's holy word is a win-win. However, even nature teaches us that there is a consequence for every action. Therefore, I believe that it is a very risky undertaking to tempt fate by disregarding the Bible and refusing to believe that it is the holy word of God.

As true Christians, we should revere God more than anything and choose to have unwavering faith in Him, even to the point of seeming crazy in the eyes of others. We should respect the laws and ideas that God has laid out for us because He is our creator and ultimately knows what is best for us. We should not question the wisdom of God but appeal to Him for mercy toward those who question His authority out of ignorance. We should have faith in Jesus when He says that He came that we may have and live more abundant lives, despite Satan's attempt to kill, steal, and destroy everything that God wants to give us. If we trust wholeheartedly in the power of Almighty God, we will experience true peace of mind. God is the giver of all good things, and as long as we do His will, we are heirs to His promises. On the other hand, if we are willful and disobedient, this can result in all kinds of unnecessary hardships in our lives. God is just, and there are repercussions for every disobedient or willful act, some harsher than others. However, just as we are with our own children, discipline is for the ultimate good of the child. As Christians, some of us act like spoiled brats; we mess up willfully just because we know that our Father is merciful. However, we should be mindful of our reckless ways. Galatians 6:7: "Do not be deceived, God is not mocked; for whatever a man sows, that he will also reap."

Sincere Service to God is Spiritually Nourishing

In John 4:34, Jesus says, "My food is to do the will of Him who sent Me, and to finish His work." This suggests that the believer can receive true sustenance simply by doing God's will. This premise about putting God and the things of God first, which inadvertently leads to all of one's needs being met, is further solidified in Luke 12: 29-31, which encourages believers to "seek first the kingdom of God, and all these things shall be added to you." Jesus' disposition and ministry epitomized this premise to the point where He seemed to have little or no regard for His own wellbeing.

During His walk on Earth, Jesus spent most of His time among those who needed healthcare, food, spiritual deliverance, and liberating insight that comes from knowing and applying God's word. I imagine that after the countless hours of dealing with these needs, Jesus would feel extremely drained. However, His solution was never to take an extended vacation or stay away from the people who needed Him in favor of relaxing or overindulging in selfish pleasures. Instead, He used most of His time away from the crowd to spend quality time with God (Matthew 14:13 & 23; Mark 1:35; Luke 6:12; John 8:1; John 10:40). This rejuvenated Him and enabled Him to continually and unfailingly meet the needs of the crowd and do the will of our heavenly Father. Does this mean that Christians should never take vacations or do enjoyable things? No, it does not! It means that true Christians should spend most of their time in the presence of God or doing the things that please God. It further implies that certain things should be done in moderation or at opportune times, especially when they are self-serving and do very little to advance the kingdom of God.

As I alluded to earlier, it is natural to feel drained or as if the weight of the world has landed on your shoulders after spending time with non-believers or people who seem clueless about the power of God. However, as Paul says, "I discipline my body and bring it under subjection, lest when I have preached to others, I, myself should become disqualified" (1 Cor. 9:27). So, staying away from the non-believer, the poor, or the needy for a time to study, fast, and pray for strength is recommended and indeed commendable. However, when we stay away from those who are oppressed due to a total lack of concern or out of a subconscious fear of becoming burdened with the same conditions, then we are not living a life of true victory, because such behavior negates the power and will of God.

The Holy Spirit, who dwells in every born-again believer, is our Helper and was not sent so that we can select or favor certain tasks and then claim that we are doing the will of Almighty God. The Holy Spirit was sent so that we can overcome the world in every sense of the word. Therefore, we must nurture the Holy Spirit by spending time in the presence of God. All four gospels reveal that after spending long hours with the multitudes, meeting an immense variety of needs, and being confronted by all manner of contrary spirits, ideas, and habits, Jesus was often tired. However, there is no record of His complaints, and He never told His disciples to send the crowds away. Instead, He constantly had compassion on the people and scolded the disciples for trying to keep the people from coming to Him. Jesus knew what He was sent to accomplish on Earth, and He remained true to His calling and purpose. Some might argue that Jesus is the Son of God; therefore, He could do and endure anything. However, Jesus walked this earth in corruptible flesh. He had human feelings, and the Bible records instances where He slept, ate, cried, got tired, and felt overwhelmed just like we do. However, the weapon or remedy that allowed Jesus to constantly be ready to deal with the needs of the people is that He took time away from the crowd to pray, refresh Himself, and bask in the presence of the Lord. It is imperative to note that we as believers have no excuse for doing anything less outstanding than what Jesus did when He was on earth. After all, in John 14:12, Jesus declares, "Most assuredly, I say unto you, he who believes in Me, the works that I do he will do also; and greater works than these he will do, because I go to my Father."

Follow the Examples Set by Our Lord and Savior

I am emphatic in my belief that there is a lesson in everything that Jesus did. As Christians, we need to follow these examples because Jesus came to show us how to please God as well as how to live victoriously. There are valuable lessons we can learn from Jesus. He helped others despite the risk of losing His own life. He ate when He was hungry, but only after He gave thanks to God. He slept during times when others were awake and worried. He rested when He was tired. He wept out of concern for His friends when He witnessed their pain. He took the time to pray and be alone with God regularly. He used God's word against every form of temptation or confrontation that He was faced with. He saw the opportunity to glorify God in every situation, and His personal needs and desires were never elevated above those of the oppressed. As born-again believers, it is wise to note that in living the way that He did, Jesus always pleased our heavenly Father. In John 8:29, Jesus said, "He who sent Me is with Me. The Father has not left Me alone, for I always do those things that please Him."

As wise disciples, we need to follow Jesus' example. Many of us are misguided in our belief that we should not spend time in the company of sinners or that when we are in the company of sinners or non-believers, we need to go out of the way to show how different or 'holy" we are. However, there is a difference between a person who has never been born again and the person who willfully disregards and dishonors the Living God. Jesus spent most of His time in the company of sinners because He wanted to share a better alternative to the life they were living. The gospels are full of accounts of sinners who came into contact with Jesus and were inspired to change their ways without Him heaping fire and brimstone upon them. As Jesus' followers, why do we endeavor to create a path of oppression for those who are already oppressed? As followers of Jesus Christ, we are called to aid in the enlightenment of those who are lost and in the liberation of anyone who is unwittingly living in darkness. However, it is wise to note that it is impossible to walk in Jesus' footsteps without first realizing that we are saved by grace and that we need "divine assistance" to love others unconditionally. Jesus knew this, so He did not leave us unarmed. He gave us the Holy Spirit to enable and empower us to have dominion over the flesh and to do the will of our Lord in the world.

When we trust in God and fortify ourselves with God's word, the Holy Spirit will continually "lift up" a Godly standard against the foolishness of the world. However, we must be deliberate and consistent in nurturing the Spirit of God within us so that we can function optimally. It is important to pray, meditate on and declare God's word regularly. It also means that as true Christians, we need to use our discretion and avoid frequenting places or engaging in activities that do nothing to enhance our spiritual growth. 1 Corinthians 15:33 warns, "Do not be deceived; evil company corrupts good habits." I must admit that the preceding Scripture seems to support the Christian who goes out of his/her way to avoid the company of sinners. However, the Christian who is grounded in Christ and knows his/her purpose for being among the sinners is alert and will never be led by them but instead seeks to be a light to those in darkness. On the other hand, the Christian who spends time in the company of other Christians or individuals who are corrupted in their ways and anti-Christ in their thought patterns can unwittingly be influenced by such individuals. Consequently, these types of interactions do nothing to advance the kingdom of heaven on earth..

Be Vigilant and Consistent in All Things Concerning God

As born-again believers, we also need to be aware of those moods or times when we do not feel like praying or studying God's word and guard against any increasing appetite for things that are morally questionable by God's standards. Satan uses these opportunities to attack or hammer at our faith, and the result of constant hammering in the natural and spiritual sense can lead to defects in structure or complete destruction. Hence, it is very critical for every born-again believer to strictly adhere to Jesus' command to "watch and pray," simply because Satan is constantly trying to kill and steal our dreams and destroy our lives by causing us to "walk in the flesh." It is our nature to walk in the flesh, and it can feel good to walk in the flesh. However, when we walk in the flesh, it is difficult to walk in Jesus' footsteps. Walking in Jesus' footsteps always results in a deeper level of satisfaction. Therefore, we are encouraged to walk in the Spirit so that our ways can please God (Galatians 5:16-26).

Many Christians today are more concerned about receiving honor or recognition from their peers rather than God. However, a true ambassador lives for Jesus Christ and portrays Christ-like character and qualities in every situation to the honor and glory of God. Jesus left the perfect example for us to follow. Therefore, we should not concern ourselves with trying to be like anyone else or worrying about what someone else says or thinks we should be doing, except when those expectations and words resonate with Jesus' mandate for our lives. Furthermore, instead of vainly pursuing selfish ambitions or personal gratification, we need to allow the Holy Spirit to mold us and help us to demonstrate Godly love and fulfill our true purpose on Earth. I believe that only what we do in Christ and for Christ will last or hold up on that day when we stand before God to give an account for our lives.

Be True Representatives of Christ in The World

As kingdom ambassadors, we must fulfill our purpose as salt and light in the world. This means that we should always strive to be a source of inspiration and answers to those who are lost or oppressed. If all the light and salt keep to themselves, they render themselves ineffective and of no use or service to God. This tells me that true Christians should never be satisfied with a ministry that is limited to the four walls of a church building. Jesus said that our righteousness should exceed that of the Pharisees. The Pharisees were a very religious group who knew the scriptures and strived to follow all the laws given by Moses. However, they were self-serving, extremely hypocritical, coldhearted, judgmental, and unforgiving. They kept to themselves and only associated with those of like mind or similar social status. Therefore, they were of no real benefit to those who were in need around them.

On the other hand, Jesus exemplified grace, demonstrated love, and showed compassion to those who needed the True Physician. Therefore, as believers, we must avoid the company or counsel of those who are blatantly unforgiving and deliberately merciless, not only because bad company corrupts but also because Jesus desires "mercy rather than sacrifice" (Matthew 9:13). Instead, we should be intent on blazing trails that help in the liberation and empowerment of those with various needs, because, in so doing, we would be propelled by the same anointing that fueled Jesus' ministry on Earth.

As born-again believers, we are not expected to condone sin, but it is never our duty to judge or condemn either. We also should not allow ourselves to be governed by our selfish nature and think that once we become Christians, our only duty and purpose is to stick close to other Christians and maintain our "sanctity." If that was the case, Jesus did not need to send the Holy Spirit to dwell within us. The Holy Spirit is our teacher, comforter, support, guide, and helper as we go about emulating and finishing the work of Jesus in the world. So, if we Christians stay in our little corners and make no attempt to impact the world positively, we have no effect and are of no use to those who need salt and light. If salt stays in a bowl, will it ever season the food or fulfill its potential as a preservative? If light hides, covers itself, or stays in a room already filled with light, how can it illuminate the dark places? The Holy Spirit causes the fruit of the Spirit to manifest in our lives and therefore make us examples for those who are lost. In other words, every ambassador must let the light of Christ shine through his or her life so that those in darkness may be drawn to the light and victory that is Jesus Christ. Our light needs to be constantly visible so that those who are oppressed by darkness may not be blinded by it but rather see the light at the end of the tunnel or the silver lining behind the dark clouds and gravitate towards it. A Christian should always strive to be a source of true hope and comfort to those in need.

Be a Source of Inspiration, Love, and Relief to Others

Getting an individual to change his or her mindset from that of a victim to a victorious believer is very critical. It requires wholehearted trust and belief in the power and promises of God. As ambassadors for Christ, we are not called to enable people in their weaknesses but rather to empower them with the true knowledge of our Lord and Savior. Jesus' ministry was about spiritual enlightenment and empowerment. He proved on countless occasions (especially when He gave His life on Calvary) that He came so that we can have more abundant lives. Jesus also wanted people to know that the bondages of fear, doubt, and unbelief were not of His kingdom. Doubt, fear, and unbelief are actual vices of the kingdom of darkness meant to keep human beings spiritually blind and defeated. As believers, we must strive daily to walk in the light and liberty that Jesus died to give us.

During His ministry on Earth, Jesus pointed out that the teachings of the Pharisees were not only burdensome and self-serving but misleading. The Pharisees had a lot of ideas and traditions that Jesus observed. However, Jesus had a problem with individuals who hoarded their possessions, used their education to oppress others, or thought that their positions meant that they should be served rather than serving others. As ambassadors of Christ, we should be mindful that the kingdom of Heaven can only be advanced in the world when we deliberately use our education, possessions, and positions to help and serve others.

Jesus admonishes us in Mark 12:31 to love our neighbors as we love ourselves. If we strived to do this every day, our relationships with others and our outreach to those who are in need would be more palpable. Instead, we are still in love with ourselves, and we rarely "put ourselves in another person's shoes." It is an unequivocal guarantee that if we genuinely strived to love our neighbors like ourselves, fear would not be a deterrent to our outreach, and disdain or indifference would be absent from our interactions with those in need.

Endeavor to Live by the Golden Rule

Jesus told the parable of the Good Samaritan (Luke 10:30-37) to show us how we should treat our neighbors. Many of us go through our lives treating others like the priest in the story. We go out of our way to avoid the so-called "undesirables" in our society. Some of us think that we are too holy to get involved with these individuals. Others feel that someone else will minister to the needs of the lost. On the other hand, some of us are like the Levite in the story. There are times when our curiosity causes us to inquire into the unfortunate circumstances of others, yet we do nothing to help. We go through life blatantly aware of the less fortunate, but we are consumed with our own agendas and thoughts of our own safety or wellbeing. We rarely take the time to consider what we would want someone to do for us if the circumstances were reversed. Nonetheless, Jesus wants us to treat our neighbors in the same way that the Samaritan treated the wounded man in the story. The Samaritan had his own agenda, but he obviously did not mind putting it aside for a moment. He was not overwhelmed with thoughts of his own safety, and he did not consider himself inconvenienced to lend a helping hand. Instead, he went the extra mile to treat the wounded man, perhaps in the same way that he would have liked to be treated if the roles were reversed.

Is the "golden rule" so difficult for us to live by? Matthew 7:12 states that "whatever you want men to do to you, do also to them, for this is the Law and the Prophets." If we lived by this rule, we would all be better, more merciful, and less judgmental Christians. As born-again believers, we have our life's work cut out for us. With this commandment, "love your neighbor as yourself," every Christian can claim that he or she is called to do a special "work." Our special work is to go out of our way to try to treat everyone (including the outcasts and even our enemies) the exact way we would like to be treated if the roles were reversed. No matter what or how much we do, our labor is in vain if we do not strive to master the art of Godly love and act within its context.

Beware of Satan's Varying Devices

As believers, we also need to be mindful that when we interact with certain individuals, they can make us feel as though God still holds us accountable for our past mistakes and continues to see us shrouded in sin. We need to recognize that these individuals are being used as agents of darkness because they use their words to tear down, cause depression, or perpetuate despair. While on Earth, Jesus described Satan as the one who comes to kill, steal, and destroy. Therefore, anyone who deliberately uses his or her energy to hinder positive growth, crush another's dreams, or take credit for someone else's ideas is acting like an agent of darkness.

As human beings, we are prone to making mistakes. We constantly go back on our words, and we find ourselves doing the exact things that we try so hard not to do. However, once we become born again believers, we need to train our minds to "walk in the Spirit" so that we would not give in to the temptations of our old sinful nature. Walking in the Spirit is not automatic, but it can become second nature with consistent practice and conscious effort.

If we do not train our minds through fasting, praying, and meditating on God's word, it is easy to revert to our old ways and habits. Does this mean that the Spirit of The Lord has left us or leaves us when we make mistakes? On the contrary, the book of Isaiah (59:21) states that "My Spirit which is upon you shall not depart from you from this time and forevermore." This implies that even when believers mess up, the Holy Spirit does not leave us. However, sin relegates the Holy Spirit to a dormant or inactive position in our lives, which results in many born-again believers living as victims instead of living victoriously. A Christian who continues to live as a victim cannot please God. Instead, he or she negates the power of God and, unfortunately, will ultimately be denied entry into the kingdom of God. So, we must unceasingly strive to walk in the Spirit so that we can please God in everything that we do.

Be Relentless in Tending to Your Spirit Man

Let us take a moment to consider our spirit man and our old sinful nature as seeds that are planted in the garden of our hearts. The spirit man requires careful tending and constant nurturing so that it can thrive, but our old sinful nature is like an undesirable weed that grows, whether it is encouraged or not. The weed of our old sinful nature necessitates constant trimming and plucking up so that it would not choke or stifle the desirable plant and fruit of the Holy Spirit. Therefore, as born-again believers, we must constantly and untiringly tend the garden of our hearts by avoiding words, thoughts, and actions that encourage weed-like growth and tendencies. Instead, we need to apply constant and deliberate effort into tending the rare and delicate seed of the Holy Spirit, which can only thrive when all conditions are just right. If not watered by fervent prayer, pruned by faithful application of God's word, and exposed to the sunlight of constant gratitude and praise, the Holy Spirit will never manifest Its full power in our lives. Therefore, we need to be mindful that if we do not apply any effort or attention to tending the garden of our hearts wherein grows the potentially powerful seed of the Holy Spirit, our hearts will become overgrown with the undesirable weeds of our old sinful ways.

Lean on Christ consciously and deliberately; it is in Him that we live and have our being. If we take our eyes of Christ at any time, we will lose our source of strength as well as our ability to overcome evil. As born-again believers, we need to remember that despite all our conscious efforts, weeds will still try to grow among the desired fruit of the Spirit. However, being constantly aware means taking precautions against the weeds of sin by meditating on the word of God, which prevents sin from taking root and reigning in our lives.

It is Crucial That We Stay Connected to God Our Source

As true Christians living in a corrupt world, we need to be a compelling example and a magnetic force to those who are still in darkness. No matter how adverse the situation, God will always give us the grace to shine if we remember to lean on Him. Always be aware and alert and never give Satan any room to steal God's glory. We should remember that the more adverse the situation is, the better the opportunity for God's glory to be revealed. God promised that He would never leave us nor forsake us and that He would never place more upon us than we can bear. So, when we experience any form of adversity (such as terminal diseases, disabilities, loss of a loved one, dysfunctional relationships, or severely inadequate financial resources), we should not doubt God or think that He has forsaken us. Instead, we should remember to look heavenward and trust that the One who gives us all good things will also see us through our "darkest hour."

As Christians, we should be in constant communication with our Heavenly Father. Time alone with God is indeed a necessary and fortifying experience. We need to listen to the still small voice of the Holy Spirit, which is constantly battling the desires of the flesh, and stop letting our busyness with the cares of this world distract us. The "weapons of our warfare are indeed not carnal" (2 Corinthians 10:4), and a Christian who is distracted with the cares of this world loses many battles of the mind frequently throughout the day. In Philippians 4:8, Paul, in his inspired wisdom, advised the believers to feast on spiritual food by meditating on things that are true, noble, just and pure, because this allows the Holy Spirit to "raise up" a standard when the enemy tries to attack and poison our minds with hatred, jealousy, fear, and doubt.

As true believers, we also need to be aware of the effectiveness of the "garment of praise" against the "spirit of heaviness." If we are assailed with feelings of sadness or despair, we ought to pray and praise our way through. Singing praises and chanting the word of God causes the spirit of heaviness to leave us. We should constantly sing praises unto God because it is an ointment that repels Satan and disarms his minions. Praise is a weapon that believers need to use every day and in every situation. Praise keeps us near to God, and it keeps the oppression of Satan at bay. The Bible teaches us that God inhabits the praises of His people (Psalms 22:3). So, singing praises is a way to draw near to God, and when we draw near to God, He will draw near to us (James 4:8). Furthermore, Psalm 16:11 confirms that in the presence of the Lord, there is fullness of joy. Therefore, I wholeheartedly recommend to every believer that the tried-and-true remedy for overcoming spiritual heaviness is to "put on the garment of praise." So, no matter how severe the emotional or psychological battle may be, drag yourself to a place of reprieve where you can "get your praise on!"

For more Scriptural study related to this chapter, go to page 125.

CHAPTER 4

Appealing to The Heart of God

Understanding Our Purpose as Believers

As true believers, it is prudent to recognize that we have but one true purpose in this life. Our purpose is to perpetuate the principles of the kingdom of Heaven throughout the world. This means that we must constantly and deliberately let the Christ in us shine through us as much as possible. Consequently, those in darkness would see and receive the light and learn to live the victorious lives that Jesus died to purchase for every believer. When we fulfill this purpose, all of our desires, needs, and wants are inadvertently met in this world and in the world to come. If we operate under the right principles, we can indeed have our cake and eat it, too. As representatives of the Lord God Almighty, we have a mission, and God promises that He will take care of our every need as long as we follow and carry out His instructions. Our interests, our aims, and our desires should always be to do what would please Him. It is in God that we have our being. He made us; we did not create ourselves. Therefore, once we return from our sinful rebellion, we should humbly recognize and accept that every law, command, and statute that Our Creator ever gave was for the ultimate benefit of humanity. Furthermore, since we know that the heart and mind of Our Heavenly Father are always on the welfare of His children, we should act like responsible and compassionate children consistently striving to help our spiritual siblings who are still lost.

As children of The Creator, we must also recognize certain facts. God knows everything about us. He knows what causes us to malfunction, so He warns against those things. God knows how to fix anything that ails us. There is nothing so difficult, unusual, or perplexing about the spiritual, emotional, physiological, intellectual, psychological, or physical aspects of our lives that God can't handle. As a matter of fact, the Creator's manual, which is the Bible, is filled with examples of situations and lessons about the way God would have us deal with specific situations. In all things and in every situation, trust God and have faith in the power of God, and He will deliver you and provide for you every time. The Bible shows us the unnecessary hardships, disappointments, and heartaches that humans experience because of rebellion and lack of adherence to the will of God. As human beings, we regularly test God with our willfulness and presumptuous ways. We take for granted that God is forgiving, merciful, loving, and kind, and we continually disregard His directions for abundant living. Nonetheless, God has given clear instructions about the benefits that come from following His manual (the Bible) as well as the consequences of improper usage or disregard of direct commands.

God is Aware of Everything

Humans may act foolish and disrespectful sometimes and try to challenge God, blame God, or question His ways, but the truth is, no one has or ever will win a case against God. No one can ever be wiser than God or understand the ways of God enough to reject entirely the acknowledgment of the Higher Being, which is Almighty God. According to Isaiah 55:8, "For My thoughts are not your thoughts, neither are your ways My ways says the Lord. For as the heavens are higher than the earth, so are My ways higher than your ways, and my thoughts than your thoughts." Therefore, true wisdom is to acquiesce to the power of God over our lives and in the world around us. In hindsight, Satan now knows that he made a colossal error to dare contend with God or try to usurp authority in Heaven. He knows that he is doomed for eternity, and in his frenzy, he is upset and determined to mislead, corrupt, and destroy whoever leaves themselves open to his deception. Frankly, the Devil hates God! Therefore, his aim is to spite God by misleading humankind to spend eternity with him in hell. However, he can try with all his might to win, at the good humor of Almighty God, but evil will never prevail in the presence of true goodness and light. The light that emanates from the throne of the Lord God Almighty is so blinding that evil and darkness will eventually be totally destroyed.

Does God care about the ills that take place in this world? Most certainly! It is a part of our Heavenly Father's nature to care for His children. Our sinful nature constantly causes us to defy God, disobey Him, and show little or no regard for Him or His ways. If God did not love us or care about what happens to us, humankind would have been destroyed a long time ago. Yet, God does not and will never force His will upon us, and He certainly cannot live for us. However, He does provide a way of escape, and it is His desire to see all His children receive the gift of eternal life, which is in His Son Jesus Christ. However, we must remain mindful that when we choose to walk contrary to the will of the Lord, we reap the curses of a world that has been corrupted by Satan.

What do you think about the following trends of humanity? Instead of choosing life, we choose death. Instead of choosing abundance and peace of mind in Christ, we choose the mere appearance of these things. Instead of choosing love and the Father of love, we choose deception and the father of lies. As Christians, we must remain vigilant and work diligently to help free our brothers and sisters from the oppression of deceit and from the trends that lead to heartache and, ultimately, death.

God Our Heavenly Father

Let's consider for a moment how an earthly father may love his children and want to provide permanent and continual protection for them. He gives his children boundaries and instructions that will ensure that they regularly experience his love and protection. It makes him feel good to provide security and protection for his children. However, if these children stray, disregard, and forget these instructions, they leave themselves open to harm, heartaches, and hardships. When harm befalls them, their father is often not at liberty to do much about it.

Let's further consider a scenario where a rebellious child returns home and the father receives the child with open arms. In some cases, even though the father is willing to lay aside his disappointment and forgive the child for constant, willful straying, the father may decide that the best lesson is to leave that child to reap the results of his or her contrary ways. This is often done out of tough love because the father realizes that he is not doing the child any favors by constantly providing a means of escape when the child seems determined to be destroyed along with everyone or everything along the way. However, if that child is genuinely repentant and reforms from contrary ways, the father will never turn his child away. At times, depending on the extent to which that child has strayed, the father may be a little hesitant to fully restore that child's status/inheritance without first testing his or her stability. Therefore, the sooner that child proves a commitment to reformed living, the sooner that child will be able to reap the rewards of complete reinstatement. Similarly, when we become Christians and prove to be faithful and diligent in the things that God desires of us, we become the beneficiaries of all the promises and blessings that our Father reserves for His children.

So, do we have hard times when we stray and disregard the counsel of our earthly fathers? Certainly! Does it grieve the hearts of our fathers? Definitely! Do you think our fathers ever stop hoping and praying for our reformation and deliverance? Never! Do our fathers want to protect us and provide security for us? Always! So how does the mass heartache or struggle between the loving father and the beloved child begin? Well, it's simple; we love to test our limits and experience things for ourselves. We love to do things our way or simply rebel against boundaries that are ultimately set for our own benefit. Some of us think that boundaries are too restrictive. We assume that we know better than our fathers, and so we set out to prove it. Many of us want to get our inheritance on our terms, and we want to make deals, take short cuts, and still expect to get the same rewards as those who are obedient and follow the wise counsel of their fathers.

Unconditional Love and Forgiveness

Let us now consider the story that Jesus told about the prodigal son in Luke 15:11-32. In this story, the father had two sons. The younger son decided that he would disregard all that his father had done and provided for him over the years. He repaid his father for his kindness by taking his inheritance and going in pursuit of vain and selfish pleasures. This inheritance was one that he did not earn but was privileged to, simply because he was born into the family. Nonetheless, the loving father, who wanted nothing more than to give his sons the desires of their hearts, gave the younger son his inheritance, even though it grieved his heart to do so. His son was going away and would no longer be under his protection, so, to him, he was losing a son. However, the older son decided to stay at home and work with his father. The older son remained under his father's protection. His father always knew where he was and, no doubt, considered him to be a very loyal, dependable, and trustworthy son. So, everything that his father had belonged to him.

However, in his dutifulness, the older son may have somehow forgotten about his inheritance and thought that he had to prove himself further or wait for an appointed time before he could happily partake in his inheritance. Perhaps the older son was enjoying his status and the benefits of his position all along. Either way, selfish human nature, jealousy, or an unforgiving heart made it difficult for him to appreciate the return of his younger brother. Therefore, he was upset when he noticed how much his father celebrated the return of his younger brother. He was unwilling to accept that his father could forgive and forget all that his younger brother had done and that he could simply revel that his son had returned to the fold before it was too late. If the older son was paying attention, he would have noticed that it had grieved his father to have his younger son out in the world without his protection.

The older son proved to be loyal and dependable in his ways, but he would have pleased his father even more if he knew where his father's heart was. His father's heart was on the condition and welfare of his lost son. If he knew his father's heart, the older son could have gone after his younger brother and somehow convinced him to return home so that he would not have endured the substandard lifestyle that resulted from his rebellion. As believers, we know that the youngest son represents the lost (non-believer) and the older son represents the believer. In this story, both the believer and the non-believer had some faults. However, by telling the story in this way, Jesus wanted Christians to realize that Our Heavenly Father is pleased with our loyalty and dutiful ways, but we truly touch His heart when we operate in the spirit of love and forgiveness and declare the good news of the gospel, causing the "lost sheep" to return to the fold. No matter how many sheep are safe in the fold enjoying the benefits of the abundant life, our Father is deeply concerned about those who are not safe and those who are still lost. Therefore, we must diligently work the fields to help save the lost. We cannot allow jealousy, resentment, or unforgiveness to overshadow our ability to be happy for others and wholeheartedly celebrate with those who are finally freed from oppression.

God Cares Deeply for The Lost

It is not God's will or desire to see even one soul perish. His desire is to save humankind, the favored element of creation, from the wages of sin, which is death. Therefore, He sent His only begotten Son not only to die for the sins of the world but also to make fishers of men. Now that Jesus has died and returned to Heaven to prepare a place for all who believe in Him, it is God's desire to see His children take advantage of the gift of eternal life. God's heart, mind, and eyes are always on those who are lost, oppressed, or less fortunate. Therefore, we are always close to God's heart when we help those in need, feed the lost sheep, and become active fishers of men by telling others about Jesus, who is The Way, The Truth, and The Light.

Have you noticed how effortless it is to get busy doing "good works"? As ambassadors, we do not get to select what we will do to honor God. Instead, we must do the will of our Heavenly Father. We cannot make the mistake that Jonah made (Jonah chapter

1) and decide if, where, or when we would obey God. Rest assured that if God sends us anywhere, He will provide for us and take care of us. God cannot lie. If He promises a reward or a consequence as it relates to a specific course of action, He will see His word through. Be wise, therefore, and know that The Spirit of God will not always strive with humankind. There is a Day of Judgment and Reckoning, because God is just, and on that Day, there will be no excuse for those who harden their hearts in rebellion or unbelief. However, God is also infinitely merciful, loving, and kind. He continues to provide us with countless opportunities to repent and return from our season of rebellion. When we forsake our sinful ways and return home, we can become the recipients of all the good things that our Heavenly Father wants to lavishly bestow upon us.

As true believers who know the heart of God and His will that no human being should perish, we should work fervently to help bring the light of the gospel to those who are lost and living in darkness. We would indeed please our Heavenly Father when we live, work, and serve with a heart of love. When we seek out and help to save the lost, causing them to turn to God and recognize that God is our all, we would be fulfilling our purpose as agents of the kingdom of Heaven.

We should always remember and remind others that it is our Heavenly Father's good pleasure to meet our every need and crown us with His mark and Sovereign protection. God wants to see all of His children live happy and purpose-filled lives. Our mission is to appeal to the heart of God by surrendering to Him and endeavoring to be His hands and feet in the world. We are meant to provide the caring hugs, the shoulder to lean on, the listening ear, the understanding nod, the loving embrace, the hot meal, the warm clothes, the message of forgiveness, and anything else that is required by the lost, needy, and oppressed around us. If we trust God, He will endow us with whatever it takes to do these things for His precious lost children. Furthermore, in eternity, He promises to reward those who take time out to be His hands and feet in this world (Matthew 25:34-36).

Revering and Trusting Our Heavenly Father

In all things, we need to remember that God is our Creator. Therefore, we need to be careful not to provoke or anger the heart of God. He created us for a specific purpose. So, for us to experience the abundant life that He promised us, we must do His will. It is indeed foolish to act as though we have ultimate control over our lives and know for certain that we could gain eternal life by some alternative means other than through our Lord and Savior Jesus Christ. It is foolish to question God and doubt His ability. God is our King, and we are His subjects; we must be humble and submit to His will, whether or not we understand it or appreciate it. Let us be careful not to regard our Heavenly Father the way we sometimes disrespect and disregard our earthly fathers, acting as if we can do a better job or that we know how best to handle a situation. It is not wise to contend with or rebel against God. God graciously allows us to present our cases, but we should not get carried away with the belief that God is limited or short of ideas. God would not, has not, and will never lower His standards to please anyone. The truth is, God has extended His grace towards humankind to please Himself. It pleases God to provide a way of escape for His children. However, we need to be aware of and take advantage of this Way of escape from death and eternal damnation. Yes, be ever mindful that Jesus is our Way of escape!

As I alluded to earlier, it is not God's will that any man should perish, but that we all would come to the knowledge of the great heritage that is ours in and through Jesus Christ. Jesus was sent to redeem us back to God. Jesus' death is indicative of God's great love for humankind, His unchanging regard for our souls, and His high standard of commitment toward our redemption. Therefore, let us not question God's grace or take it for granted, but instead live lives of love and gratitude toward Him. Ever since humanity's fall in the garden, humans have done everything possible to get further away from God at the expense of their only souls. Humankind has repeatedly gotten into situations and has experienced circumstances and consequences that are a direct result of disobedience to God. Nonetheless, when we repent and accept Christ into our hearts, God forgives us and gives us a new lease on life. The only thing God requires is our acceptance of the gift of salvation through Christ Jesus and our obedience, as well as our trust in Him, so that we can continue to receive all good things in Jesus' name.

From the beginning, God has been showing us His heart and teaching us the benefits of obedience and trust in Him. If we trust Him, He will take care of our every need. If we trust Him, He will fight for us. If we trust Him, He will be our healer. If we trust Him, He will be our strength. If we trust Him, He will give us the desires of our hearts. If we trust Him, He will give us the right words to say. If we trust Him, He will cause favor to follow us wherever we go. If we trust Him, He will make us prosperous. If we trust Him, He will provide a way of escape. If we trust Him, He will give us wisdom. If we trust Him, He will contend with the enemy on our behalf. If we trust Him, He will give us the courage to stand up against Satan and his demonic army. If we trust Him, He will provide us with a way back to Him. If we trust Him, He will give us the Holy Spirit, which is His power, love, wisdom, wholeness, and authority to help us live victoriously and have dominion in this world.

Service That is Close to Our Father's Heart

As believers who are truly aware of God's goodness and what He has in store for those who serve Him, it is our duty to help the lost to come to this marvelous light. Let us always be mindful that no matter how much good we do or how busy we may get, we are never close to the heart of God unless we engage in a specific kind of work. In John 21:14-17, Jesus asked Peter three times if He loved Him, and when Peter affirmed this, Jesus told him the way to translate this love into meaningful work. Therefore, it is indisputable that our love for God requires us to engage in ministry that provides spiritual as well as physical food for those in need. As followers of Christ, we are His sheep, and He is the Good Shepherd. In John 10:16, Jesus states, "And other sheep I have which are not of this fold; them also I must bring, and they will hear My voice; and there will be one flock and one shepherd." Many of the sheep that Jesus is referring to include individuals from diverse backgrounds, nationalities, religions, cultures, races, and belief systems. However, it also includes people who are close to us, such as the poor, the orphans, the sick, the widows, and those who are spiritually oppressed, or actually imprisoned.

For many Christians, the aforementioned is indeed not glamorous work, but it is the meaningful work that keeps us in the will of God and close to the heart of God. In Matthew 25:34-37, we see that when Jesus returns on the day of reckoning, He will reward those who did His will on earth. In this passage of Scripture, the obedient are referred to as sheep, and those who ignored the will of God are referred to as goats. It is crucial to note what is said of the obedient sheep who inherit the kingdom: "For I was hungry and you gave Me food, I was thirsty and you gave Me drink; I was a stranger and you took Me in; I was naked and you clothed Me; I was sick and you visited Me; I was in prison and you came to Me." Furthermore, in Luke 14:13-14, Jesus says, "But when you give a feast, invite the poor, the maimed, the lame and the blind. And you will be blessed, because they cannot repay you; for you shall be repaid at the resurrection of the just." Therefore, as true believers who endeavor to touch the Father's heart and fulfill the mandate of Christ, we must work fervently to be of service and a blessing to anyone (far or near) who is lost or held captive by various forms of spiritual or physical oppression.

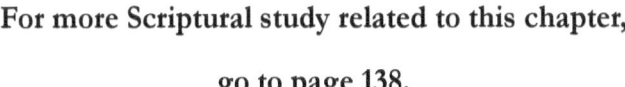

For more Scriptural study related to this chapter,

go to page 138.

CHAPTER 5

The Error of Our Ways

Recognizing the Amazing Gift We Have in Jesus

In John 12:46, Jesus says, "I have come as a light into the world, that whoever believes in me should not abide in darkness." In the book of Mark 2:17, Jesus also states that "those who are well have no need of a physician, but those who are sick. I did not come to call the righteous, but the sinners to repentance." These scriptures make it clear that Jesus did not come to do away with God's high standard of living for His children, but rather to extend God's mercy toward all humanity and to provide a source of enlightenment and the way of escape from eternal damnation.

When Jesus gave His life on Calvary, this was an eternally sufficient sacrifice for all our sins. His sacrifice and obedience also make it possible for every human being, regardless of lineage or heritage, to be adopted into the family of God. It is through the bloodline of Jesus Christ that all humankind can become a chosen people, exemplifying the kingdom of God on earth. It also means that all human beings have equal opportunity to become a chosen people, set apart, and joint-heirs to the promises of God. Jesus' sacrifice made it possible that through His interminable bloodline, all of humanity can experience the blessings and the favor of God in their lives. Did Jesus do away with the covenant that God made between Abraham and his seed? Absolutely, not! What Jesus did was extend the hand of mercy, first to the Jews (who were now deserving of death because of their constant rebellion and stiff-necked ways) and then to the Gentiles who were not descendants of Abraham and destined to die in sin. Such a selfless sacrifice makes it in poor taste for any individual or group to act as if they have a monopoly on God's favor and blessings. Jesus' sacrifice makes it incumbent for every true Christian to share this good news, not for personal gain, but out of sheer gratitude for the supremely amazing and remarkable way that God orchestrated and delivered salvation's plan to the world.

Love and Trust Should be Our Response

As Christians, mercy should be our default mode of operation as it relates to dealing with others. In other words, if we want to continue pleasing God, our words and actions need to be constantly motivated by genuine love and should involve some degree of self-sacrifice. Self-sacrifice means forgoing a personal need or desire and laying aside personal feelings for the benefit of anyone in need, even someone considered to be an enemy. Jesus has called us to be generous, self-sacrificing individuals and to trust His promise that if we lose anything for His or the gospel's sake, that we will reap the rewards in this life and in the world to come. Therefore, it is risky to hoard our possessions and live selfishly because it could ultimately result in the loss of everything valuable to us, including our very souls. We should also be mindful that "unless God keeps the house, the watchman watches in vain" (Psalm 127:1). So, rather than spending so much time guarding and trying to preserve our earthly possessions, we should do the will of God and trust Him to help us take care of everything else. Furthermore, we cannot let the pursuit of wealth distract us to the point where we neglect our relationship with God and forget about our responsibility to those in need.

Trust God with all that you have, and He will take care of you. It takes crazy faith to bank on the promises of the Unseen God, but who will you trust above the Creator of heaven and earth? When God delivers you from bondage and oppression, who do you think needs to hear your testimony? Would your testimony be of more benefit to someone who has been delivered in much the same way? Or would it be more beneficial to someone who is still seeking to be delivered? If your answer is the latter, then tell me why do Christians like to testify among themselves so much more than they like to share with those who are lost and afflicted? I have often wondered of what benefit is a light if it is already in a place filled with light, or of what benefit is salt if it stays in a box. To have real impact, light must be put in a place where there is darkness, and then the light will stand out and shine. In the same way, salt must be used and sometimes mixed with other ingredients so that it can serve its purpose. However, when testifying to the lost or afflicted, we need to be careful not to appear boastful or offensive in any way. It should always be our intent and desire to use our testimonies to encourage others to keep the faith and never stop trusting in God.

Walking in Jesus' Footsteps with Humility

As citizens of the kingdom, we should not get caught up in the trap of labeling people as "sinners," and we certainly should not elevate ourselves to sit in judgment of others. We have all sinned and fallen short of the glory of God. However, by grace we are saved, and through God's word and the Holy Spirit, we are blessed with the opportunity to walk in the Spirit and not fulfill the lusts of the flesh. We are daily confronted with many instances where we fall short or would sin if we do not consciously and deliberately make-up our minds to "walk in the spirit." Walking in the Spirit can become the reality of any Christian who fasts regularly, prays constantly, and studies the word of God consistently. Walking in the Spirit also requires us to meditate on Godly things and avoid spending too much time focusing on things that do nothing to nurture the Holy Spirit as an active and prominent part of our daily endeavors.

Our purpose is to continue with Jesus' mission, which is to seek and save the lost by spreading the good news of the Gospel, which is God's grace and mercy towards humankind. With the Spirit and power of God within us, it is almost sacrilegious for us to be immobilized by fear or plain disregard for others. We should not think that the world is so dangerous and times have changed so much that we would be stupid to risk our lives to help people we do not know, or that once our families are safe, we are doing okay. We should also not be deceived into thinking that as citizens of the kingdom of God, our only purpose is to save our own souls and make sure that we stay saved. Such thoughts have been perpetuated by Satan himself, because he is a liar and his main goal is to keep us selfish, self-serving, and ineffective in the kingdom of God. We need to remember that Jesus came to teach us how to be selfless and compassionate toward others and to exceed the righteousness of the Pharisees, not so that we can boast, but that we may be called true children of God. When we look at our world today, a Pharisee would be equivalent to anyone or any prevailing idea that is self-serving, full of self-righteousness, and has an overly critical or indifferent attitude towards others.

Convenient Service

Spending quality time with our families, going to church, and working in the church edifice is always recommended and is indeed a commendable thing. However, we are called to be a light to the world and to be salt on the earth. Therefore, as true believers, we must do more than required or acceptable in society or among fellow Christians. We should not be satisfied with the mere busying of ourselves with things, people, places, or activities that appear important but have no real significance in the kingdom of God. We must do all that we can to be a light to those who are living in darkness wherever we go and with whatever we do. We must do as much as possible to help individuals with their spiritual and physical needs. I am reminded of the Scripture in James 2:15; "If a brother or sister is naked and destitute of daily food, and one of you says to them, 'Depart in peace, be warmed and filled,' but you do not give them the things which are needed for the body, what does it profit?" Therefore, as disciples of Christ, we must make a deliberate and consistent effort to be more useful and relevant to those who are in "real" need. We must also operate in the spirit of true humility and be careful not to act as though we are superior or perfect, especially when we are witnessing to or helping those individuals who are already acutely aware of their own imperfections.

As true believers, we have been called to impact and infect the world with the love, mercy, forgiveness, and power of Almighty God. Nonetheless, Satan has perpetuated such a prevailing spirit of fear that many Christians believe that the world is an unsafe place and the best thing to do is stay inside, lock their doors, and make sure that what they have is protected. Do you not see the joke in this matter? Satan is laughing at many people who call themselves Christians today. We have been deceived into behaving exactly as Jesus said that we must not. Some have become steeped in logic and argue that times have changed and that it is too dangerous to share with and try to help the lost in our communities. Instead of looking at the lost with the compassion that Jesus had, many of us look upon them with disdain or fear. We judge them and condemn them instead of laboring to enlighten them. Some of us think that these are the sinners that Jesus wants us to be set apart from. However, we have been admonished to avoid the company of anyone who is called a "brother" (someone who knows better) but chooses to live a contrary life. "The lost" that we must seek out are those who are oppressed and live in ignorance relative to their God-given status on earth, re-established through Jesus' sacrifice on Calvary. Our "God-given status" is that we are children of God, who are meant to reign over the darkness in this world through the blood, power, and name of our Lord and Savior Jesus Christ. It is our great commission to preach and live the good news of this gospel so that those in darkness would be drawn to the liberating light of salvation.

The Effects of Original Disobedience

Sickness, diseases, jealousy, hatred, selfishness, unfaithfulness, pride, idolatry, lack, poverty, death, and sexual immoralities are all side effects or components of a kingdom that has nothing to do with the will of God. When God placed Adam in the Garden of Eden, He gave Adam dominion over everything that was created before him. When God presented Eve to Adam as a helpmeet, she was his partner to help fulfill God's plan to replenish the earth with God-fearing offspring. Adam and Eve were in perfect health and had no need for anything. Their purpose was to be obedient and to trust God for anything they needed. God intended to commune with them regularly and to have a very close relationship with them. According to Genesis chapter 3, after Adam and Eve had sinned, they hid because they knew God would come to them in the cool of the day to spend time in their company. They had the opportunity to be close to God every day of their lives. However, God is Holy, and no sin can enter His presence. Therefore, when Adam and Eve sinned, they were no longer allowed to enjoy the presence of The Lord regularly. Their decision to sin caused them to inadvertently lose the best thing that they could ever have experienced.

Adam and Eve's disobedience opened the doorway to perpetual sin, which is the alternate reality that was created by Satan. Adam and Eve immediately regretted their decision to disobey God. The knowledge of good and evil changed the playing field and the rules of the game of life forever. They would never again know what it meant to be innocent. They were now accountable for every decision made, word uttered, or action committed from that moment, and their descendants are subjected to the same reality.

When Adam and Eve destroyed the gift of innocence that God had given them, they opened what could be termed the proverbial "Pandora's Box." By giving room to Satan, they inadvertently and unknowingly allowed his standard of existence to enter the world. Had they ignored Satan, this unsavory display of uncertainty, sickness, death, poverty, destruction, hatred, jealousy, and similar maladies would never have become the reality of the world that God had intended for the creatures that He made in His image. God rules and reigns in heaven, and as His children, He intended us to rule and reign on Earth just like He does in heaven.

Irresponsibly Casting Blame

Have you noticed the absurd trend in the world today? Some people think that they have a right to blame God for all the evil that is happening in the world. However, God is not evil, and no evil thing can proceed from Him. The misfortunes that we suffer in this world are a direct and systematic result of a ruler who knows nothing but darkness. Keep in mind that God will punish Satan, along with every ungrateful and foolish individual who rebels against Him, for all the havoc that he has caused in the world. Nonetheless, since man's fall in the Garden of Eden, God has been giving humankind the opportunity to return to his original status of holiness and dominion. God wants us to trust Him and accept the gift of Jesus Christ as a way to get back in right standing with Him.

God offers us everything in return for wholehearted trust and obedience. As simple as that is, humankind chooses to pursue temporal things. Instead of trusting in the all-powerful, all-knowing, and all-seeing God and doing His will as outlined in His Holy word, we think that we can make deals with God and that our works somehow entitle us to every promise that God has made. However, God is, always was, and always will be God. His character is Just, Holy, and Righteous. His ways are merciful, loving, faithful, and true. His statutes are unchangeable and cannot be altered. His words always come to pass.

Nonetheless, humankind has sinned and continues to live saturated in sin. Through Satan's deception, humanity's god-like character was regrettably transformed, thus allowing sin and iniquity to have dominion over us. Therefore, when we realize that we are the unfaithful ones and that we are the ones who did not keep our end of the bargain, we should approach the "Throne of Grace" with a very humble and repentant attitude.

Realistically, we should readily acknowledge that God, in His abundant mercy, has allowed humankind to get off way too easily. Despite this, there is nothing that we can do to earn or deserve God's goodness. We are the seed of unrighteousness. We have all fallen short of the standard that God requires of us, and we cannot rectify this situation, no matter how many sacrifices we make. Does this mean that we should never attempt to make any sacrifices? Certainly, not! This simply means that whenever we make a sacrifice while doing God's work, we should check our attitude, because it is actually only because of God's grace that we are ever able to do anything. God, in all graciousness, has provided everything that we could ever need, right down to the perfect sacrifice for the eternal remission of our sins. This means that He has provided us with a way back to Him and a way to have victory over Satan's vices in the world that we live in.

Unapologetically God All by Himself

God is holy, and He is God all by Himself! He will still be God even after we die, and we can do absolutely nothing to alter this. Therefore, it does not make sense to get caught up in presumptuous sin and question God's way of doing things. The wise thing to do is to marvel that God has included us in salvation's plan and that abundant living, as well as eternal life, is ours for the taking if we believe and receive them in Jesus' name. The best way to stay in line with the will of God is to remember that we have been saved by God's grace and through His mercy.

Consequently, some of us need to humble ourselves before God and stop acting as if God is lucky to have us and must, therefore, accept us as we are. A wise believer understands what it means to be in right standing with God. We are the ones fortunate enough to have God's love and attention! God never has and never will lower His standards to suit us. Instead, He sent His Son Jesus Christ (the only One ever able to meet the standard) to die for our sins and provide us with a cloak of righteousness, which allows us to become and be called Sons of God. As Christians, this is the basis of our belief. So, if we believe this, then our lifestyles and our actions should always be geared towards honoring our Holy Father. We are fickle and always changing to please someone or something. However, God is the same God yesterday, today, and forever. His standards and ways are still the same. He is the God of all times and all seasons. He is always up to date and never outdated! So, the God in the Old Testament, who had high standards and loved decency and order, is the same God in The New Testament who reinforces decency and order. Jesus came to pay the ransom for our sins and to provide the grace which is sufficient to enable all Christians to obey God's statutes and commands.

God is Holy, and He Lowers His Standards for No One

When we think about our Holy Father and His high standards, we would realize that grace does not negate the need to follow dutiful protocol when serving the Lord. We wonder why God's presence or power is no longer felt in many of our gatherings, especially in churches and other places of worship. First of all, our "dress" and our approach to worship is based on what we like and what makes us feel good, instead of what would bring honor, glory, and recognition to God.

Second, many of the individuals who lead the worship services or deliver the message do nothing to consecrate themselves or prepare to enter the presence of a Holy God. In many instances, church has become a place for theatrics, entertainment, and self-gratifying endeavors. I believe that somehow along the way, we have confused or made interchangeable the "work" of the church with the "worship" of God. True worship is sacred! It requires consecration, reverence and the undivided devotion of those who lead or partake in it. We must remember that "God is a Spirit, and those who worship Him must worship Him in Spirit and in truth" (John 4:24).

In our varying errors, we should be ever grateful for the grace that is wrapped up in Jesus our Savior, because it is the only reason why the wrath of God has not fallen upon us as it did in Biblical times. In Genesis 4:1-7, we read the account of Cain and Abel bringing offerings to God. According to this passage, Abel's offering pleased God, but Cain's offering did not please Him. God affirmed that when we do well, our worship is accepted, but when we do not well, sin lies at the door. In this case we could assume that Cain's heart was insincere and disconnected from the worship exercise. Further, the account of Nadab and Abihu in Leviticus 10:1-4 ended tragically because these men decided to get a bit creative in their worship. In this case, these men did not respect the process of the worship exercise as ordained by God. On the other hand, the account of Uzzah in 2 Samuel 6:5-9 ended tragically as well. In this case, even though Uzzah was well intentioned and seemingly doing a good deed, he also acted outside of the worship protocols of God. In this case, the initial bad decision on the part of the leader created the opening for the unwitting tragedy among those who followed. We also know that according to 1 Samuel 13: 7-14, Saul compromised his anointing and lineage when he chose to act outside the ordained protocols of God. Each of these accounts took place within the context of worship, but God was either displeased or very offended by the acts. So, we see that true worship to God has nothing to do with the changing times, our personal feelings, creative ideas, good intentions, or outright rebellion. Rather, true worship has to do with obedience to God, revering God, and having a deep respect for the things of God. As believers, we should always endeavor to engage in true worship to our Holy Father.

However, our approach to everything has become so carnal and void of respect for our Holy God, and the things of God that those who are "worldly-minded" are very comfortable among us. However, the holy and uncompromising God, who we claim to serve, is no longer welcome or present among us, and only the residue of His power remains. The Old Testament is a very crucial part of the Bible, and all Scripture is given for our benefit. So even though Jesus' sacrifice makes some rituals and practices unnecessary today, it is incumbent for us to adhere to high standards of protocol (decency and order) in our places of worship and the valuable principles for Godly living (such as healthy lifestyles and a day dedicated to rest and worship) which keep us in right-standing with God and are ultimately for our benefit.

Contrary to the belief of many Christians, grace is not and should never be viewed as the occasion to sin. Jesus' blood completely washes away sin. It does not cover up sin, so there should be no sin lurking in our lives. Since sin is so abominable to our Holy Father, He sent His Son to die on the cross and shed His blood to cleanse us and wash away all traces of sin. Therefore, it is unwise to think that the God who abhors sin would give us a free pass to sin. In John 5:14, Jesus spoke to a man who had recently been healed by the power of God. He said, "See you have been made well. Sin no more, lest a worse thing come upon you." This makes it clear that Jesus expects us to live lives free of sin once God's grace and mercy are extended toward us.

Furthermore, it indicates that there are consequences for anyone who continues to sin willfully after experiencing God's grace. Temptations come to all of us, but the Bible teaches us that there is no temptation that befalls us except such as common to man (1 Corinthians 10: 13). Therefore, let us view grace as God's underserving ability in and over us, which allows us to resist temptation or endure a difficult situation without compromising our Christian standard of living.

Whenever I feel burdened, overwhelmed, or tested beyond my limits, I often ask God for mercy. Mercy can often bring immediate relief from a situation. So, mercy is what allows us to "tap out" and hide in Jesus whenever we feel as though we have had enough, and we cannot bear another moment of testing. However, there are some tests and situations that must be endured for a time. This is when I ask for grace to help me endure, remain gracious, resist temptation, and continue being faithful to the will of God. So, always be mindful that the more difficult the test and the more unbearable a situation or circumstance may seem, God's grace is sufficient to help us be overcomers who never "have to" give in to any form of temptation. However, if we ever unwittingly fall short in any way along life's journey, God responds with forgiveness to those with contrite hearts.

Undue Pressure

As we go about our daily lives, we will be constantly faced with a wide variety of circumstances that we must respond to in one way or another. Our perspective, in most cases, can often predetermine our state of mind, peace of mind, and the way we approach life. Some people are predisposed to worry, a negative disposition, or a pessimistic point of view. Others may seem to be a bit too nonchalant, overly idealistic, irritatingly positive, or sometimes reckless. It should be noted that both of these categories of responses are on opposite ends of the same spectrum, and neither should be the default responses of Christians.

I believe that a good default response for Christians is embodied in the words of the prayer of serenity by Reinhold Niebuhr. The prayer states, "God grant me the serenity to accept the things I cannot change, the courage to change the things I can, and the wisdom to know the difference." If Christians remained ever mindful of this prayer, it would eliminate much of the unnecessary worry, personal pressure, or wasted efforts we apply to many situations. Furthermore, courage would be applied wisely, and we would not spend valuable time testing God, debating back and forth, or trying to change those things over which we have no control. In both instances, we could end up falsely accusing God of not answering our prayers or blaming others for not helping us or putting unwanted pressure on us. Remember, we have been given free will, and we are at liberty to respond to any situation in any way we choose. So, is it really fair to blame someone if you make yourself sick, uncomfortable, or hurt yourself as a result of the way you chose to respond to a situation?

We are the light of the world. Others should be able to look at us and see what the appropriate Christian response to any situation ought to be. Therefore, we are expected to show wisdom in all things and do whatever is humanly possible to advance or move forward instead of getting caught up in making excuses and complaining about things we have no control over. As a matter of fact, you can rightly be considered insane for putting undue pressure on yourself or for applying extra worry and effort to any situation that is beyond your control. We are only required to do as much as we can, the best we can, and nothing more or less. Everything else should be left to higher human authorities or the Highest Power, which is Almighty God. As Jesus said in Matthew 11:28-30, "Come unto me, all ye that labour and are heavy laden and I will give you rest. Take My yoke upon you and learn of Me; for I am meek and lowly in heart: and ye shall find rest unto your souls. For My yoke is easy and My burden is light."

Relationship Yokes

Second Corinthians 6:14 cautions, "Be ye not unequally yoked together with unbelievers; for what fellowship hath righteousness with unrighteousness? And what communion hath light with darkness." For the early Christians, it was crucial to guard against pagan beliefs and practices as well as unbelievers who could come in and distort the truth or frustrate the unity and growth of the church. Similar words were spoken by Moses in Deuteronomy 7, where the Israelites were admonished not to form alliances with those who practiced idolatry and other pagan rituals. However, this is a very transcendent and prudent piece of Scripture that can be applied to every human relationship where peace of mind and productivity are paramount. Consequently, many individuals use this Scripture as the basis for choosing a spouse, and many pastors use it as a basis for marrying couples. For the most part, this is very commendable and should actually be encouraged as a wise and proactive action for all Christians. However, it should be noted that equally yoked in marriage has more to do with comparability and compatibility and goes much deeper than two individuals being of the same faith or simply professing to be Christians. There are many couples of the same faith, including Christian ones, who find themselves in dysfunctional homes and unhappy marriages simply because they are unequally yoked.

So, what does it mean to be yoked together? It has to do with being joined to carry out a specific task. Many farmers discovered a long time ago that when two compatible animals are yoked together, the quality of work, level of productivity, and overall atmosphere are all very good. In like manner, when two human beings with similar dreams, goals, and mission statement, join for business purposes, there is much productivity, a low rate of frustration, and very little conflict. Therefore, we expect happy homes and healthy marriages when a man and a woman with similar beliefs, character, morals, values, and Godly purposes are yoked together. We ought not to knowingly partner with any individual who will frustrate our overall progress, God-given purpose, or spiritual walk with Christ.

Meanwhile, what do you do if you are already unequally yoked in a business or personal relationship? There are several ways to move forward in these situations. In business, you can choose to buy out your partner, sell your shares to your partner, or agree to sell the business itself and divide the profit. On the other hand, you can choose to compromise, keep the business, readily accept the challenge, and try to make the best of what you have with whom you have. Similarly, when it comes to unequal yokes in marriage, you may agree to separate and rebuild with one another after a time or, in the case of irreparable damages, sever all marital ties by divorcing one another. However, wherever possible, the ideal would be to stay together, learn how to compromise, expect and accept the challenges, get to know each other, and strive to be content with one another in the sight of God and humanity. We ought to pray without ceasing for our marriages and our partners. We must trust that even when we knowingly or unwittingly end up in dysfunctional marriages, it is not God's will that we live in frustration. It is also not God's will that we take our marriage vows lightly either. So, we must have faith that God is well able to turn around any situation and work all things out for good to them that love Him (Romans 8:28).

We are called to walk and live in wisdom. Therefore, we should lead the way in making wise decisions in all business and personal relationships. This means that we ought to be extremely careful with whom we yoke ourselves. We must be mindful that, unlike those in the world, we cannot be callous or inconsiderate of others in our dealings if ever we find ourselves in less than ideal situations. As a matter of fact, we are called to pray for those who despitefully use us, bless those that curse us, turn the other cheek, endure hardships, and forgive as much as seventy times seven. It may be a little simpler to get out of business relationships because these do not entail a sacred vow. Yet, marriage involves a sacred vow until death between a man and a woman in the presence of God and humanity. For Christians, this should translate into a lifelong commitment for better or worse, even if the bad seemingly outweighs the good. Therefore, we are admonished not to be unequally yoked ultimately for our own good, contentment, and peace of mind. So, if free will causes you to ignore this word to the wise and choose otherwise, be prepared to live with the consequences, knowing that as Christians, in God's plan, divorce is not a real option.

The Glory Belongs to God

We must live lives of humility and gratitude. We should not go around boasting about what we have done, and we should never steal or try to share God's glory. This means that whenever we have a chance to testify, we should highlight that God is so good and merciful that He has given us eternal life and welcomed us into His holy family, even though we may have been unfaithful and disobedient concerning the things of God. True believers are propelled by sheer gratitude for God's goodness, and we should endeavor to do His will, not so that we can get God to do something for us or on our behalf, but simply because it is the acceptable thing to do.

As ambassadors for Christ, our testimonies should not consist of a list of things that we have endured for God's sake or the things that we have done in the name of Jesus, even though they may all be true. Furthermore, when sharing our testimonies, we need to be careful not to elevate ourselves to hero status and relegate God to the position of "faithful sidekick." Many Christians have stolen glory from God, and this is an abomination that Satan revels in. The devil is so skillful in his deceit that when he is unable to get us to commit the visually obvious sins, he sneaks in the best way he can. Humankind is ultimately self-centered and prideful, so this is the one way that Satan can cause us to fall if we are not careful and alert at all times.

While on earth, Jesus highlighted two commandments that are considered as the Great Commandments (Mark 12:29-31). The first one is, "Love the Lord your God with all of your heart soul mind and strength and all that is within you." The second one is, "Love your neighbor like yourself." Many perceive that the main reason that Jesus gave these commandments is simply to sum up the Ten Commandments, which deal with our relationship with God and others. However, the great commandments are meant to dethrone humanity's biggest idol, which is ourselves and our selfish desires. You see, it is because of humanity's selfish love and self-seeking ways that the world is headed for destruction today. However, Our Heavenly Father knows that once we learn to truly love Him and others, this would help us to become more obedient and much better stewards of the world that we live in.

The Error of Our Ways
Modern Idolatry

Humans are aware of idols that have been created by their own hands and may go about life deliberately avoiding the actual worship of these things. We make sure that we do not spend time paying homage and worshipping idols as people may have done in the past. However, there are many things that we have placed before God and persons around us. This includes our houses, land, cars, children, jobs, husbands, wives, bodies, health, money, education, and anything else we hold near and dear to us. We say that these things are not our idols, but an idol is not only a carved object that you literally worship and make sacrifices to. An idol can be anything or anyone whom we treasure, hope in, trust in, put confidence in, boast of, or find comfort in steadfastly and wholeheartedly more than Almighty God.

Am I saying that we should not appreciate the things that God has blessed us with? Absolutely, not! We should always be good stewards and thank God for the blessings we experience every day. However, we need to revere The Source rather than the provision itself. Therefore, instead of spending all of our time and effort on these things, we should use our efforts to do the will of our Father, trusting that He is indeed able to keep, protect, and preserve everything that He has blessed us with. Nonetheless, many human beings are under the spell of money, status, and substance, often at the expense and well being of others.

Since many people are aware that obsession with possessions is a type of idol worship, it means that they may not willfully engage in this type of sin. However, Satan knows this, because he was able to deceive man in the garden by subtly appealing to his favorite idol. You may have already figured out that humankind's favorite idol is none other than self! It is pride, selfishness, and self-centered ways that have been keeping humanity from total and complete obedience to the will of God. Nevertheless, our mission, as true believers, is to walk in the selfless footsteps of our Lord and Savior Jesus Christ.

Serving Like Jesus and Living in True Abundance

Many Christians resist the work that truly defines them as

disciples of Jesus Christ. Jesus was willing and did serve others rather than being served by them. Jesus sat among the sinners, sought them out, and made Himself available to those in need regularly. His life, His freedom, and His safety were threatened constantly. Yet, He carried out the will of Almighty God with little concern for His safety, trusting that God would preserve Him from harm. He also taught and exemplified a higher standard of living as a way of exceeding mere religious acts and traditions. In John 15:12 &13, Jesus admonished His disciples to love one another as He had loved them. He told them that "greater love has no man than this, than that he lay down his life for his friends." In Matthew 7:12, He advised, "do to others whatever you would have them do to you." Jesus also said in Matthew 5:44, "love your enemies and bless those who curse you and do good to those who hate you and pray for those who spitefully use you and persecute you."

I sincerely believe that God would never put us in a situation where we would have to die for our friends or sacrifice the life or well-being of a loved one just to please Him. This is made clear in the story of Abraham and Isaac (Genesis 22). Nonetheless, God searches the heart, and He knows the level of love, faith, and commitment each of us have towards Him. Wisdom is indeed the "principal thing," and we are encouraged to seek wisdom. However, I strongly recommend that Christians seek to perfect the gift of love because love surpasses all the other gifts. It is easy to sin and 'mess up' even with all the wisdom in the world, but with Godly love in our hearts, it will be very easy to please God. Godly love enables us to lay our personal doubts, feelings, fears, hindrances, concerns, and desires aside to obey God and serve others wholeheartedly.

Have you noticed how God's plan for us to enjoy a life of dominion has been misconstrued, and we have inadvertently accepted a life of oppression and subservience? Well, this reality requires us to check ourselves and question our purpose. If God did not make man to experience poverty, sickness, lack, hatred, death, or destruction, then who would benefit from man's continued oppression and substandard living? I am so glad you are paying attention now; there is only one, and his name is Satan. If we accept and buy into the great deception that God is not concerned about His children living such ill-fated realities, Satan will continue to have dominion over our lives. Fortunately for us, however, if we accept the redemption plan that God so lovingly packaged and graciously presented through our Lord and Savior Jesus Christ, we can experience abundant living in this world and look forward to eternal life in the world to come.

Abundant living requires every born-again believer to undergo a renewal of the mind. It can rightly be assumed that being born again means that we must choose to accept by faith a clean slate of innocence. In so doing, we become childlike, as Jesus says in John 3:3, "unless a man is born again, he cannot see the kingdom of God." Or when He says in Matthew 18:3, "Unless you are converted and become as little children, you will by no means enter the kingdom of heaven." Before the fall, Adam and Eve were innocent, like little children. They trusted God and depended on Him as their source for everything, in much the same way that infants depend on their parents or primary caregivers for everything. They did not lean on their own understanding, because they were not deceived and corrupted yet, and they had no point of sinful reference. They only knew and believed what God told them. There was no opportunity to sin until they started to believe and heed the words of someone other than their Source.

Childlike Innocence

As born-again believers, we would look to God and expect Him to take care of all our needs. As innocent and defenseless children of God, we would depend on Him to protect and take care of us. As obedient children of God, we would follow His commandments without question or hesitation because we would trust that He knows best and that everything He tells us is for our own good. We must realize, however, that the little children referred to in the scriptures were somewhat innocent and seemingly purer because they were not exposed to the world as it is today.

This should make us realize that we can only protect our children from Satan's destructive forces by placing them under the protection of Almighty God. As Christians, the best gift we can give our children is to be God-fearing parents. In so doing, we will raise our children right and spare them the heartaches of being slaves to the ruler of the darkness in this world.

For us to appreciate the kind of innocent mindset or the child-like faith and trust that God requires, we would have to imagine what it must have been like for Adam and Eve in the garden before any sin entered the world. In child-like innocence, Adam and Eve stood before God, naked and unashamed. They were unaware of themselves, without inhibitions, and unconscious of any wrongdoing. They trusted God and relied on Him as their ultimate source for everything. Is that not how our little ones are before they become aware of themselves and begin to question and defy the very ones who were there for them, taking care of them all the while? Nonetheless, it is the perspective of this child-like faith or innocence that leads to the level of obedience and trust in God, ultimately resulting in the abundant living that God has designed for us since the beginning of time.

For more Scriptural study related to this chapter,

go to page 146.

CHAPTER 6

Men of Vision and Purpose

Setting A Higher Standard of Living

I believe that it would be prudent for all men, as male ambassadors for Christ, to aspire to be like bishops if only as a means of setting and emulating a standard of living that would always please God. Titus 1:7-9 states that, "a bishop must be blameless, as a steward of God, not self-willed, not quick tempered, not greedy for money, but hospitable, a lover of what is good, sober-minded, just, holy, self-controlled, holding fast the faithful word as he has been taught, that he may be able, by sound doctrine, both to exhort and convict those who contradict." A similar passage of Scripture is found in 1 Timothy 3:1-7.

If all men lived by these standards, then character flaws and unsavory tendencies such as infidelity, lack of integrity, partiality in judgment, misappropriation of finances, fickle identity, weak-mindedness, narcissism, and outright lack of Godly standards would not be so prevalent among males today. I wholeheartedly believe that men of God should continually keep these qualities and standards at the forefront of their minds and deliberately practice them daily so that exemplary lifestyles would be their default mode. Furthermore, if every male aspired to be like a bishop or considered himself to be in training by biblical standards, regardless of his status in society, there would be far less dysfunctional families, useless churches, deteriorating government systems, and depraved societies.

Humility and Accountability

As enlightened men of God, it is time to 'man-up' and start being more accountable, conscious, and responsible members of society. However, you must always be careful not to act like an authority unto yourselves. You were chosen as the head of the home and the head of the church, but Christ is head over you. You can do nothing in and of yourselves because your authority comes from God. It is also wise to avoid the sin of presumption, because God does not need man in order to be God. However, to be a real man, every man needs God. As a servant of God, it is in your best interest to follow God's commands. God is no respecter of persons, and He requires total obedience and accepts no deviations when it comes to carrying out His orders. God loves us and shows faithful mercy towards us, but there are always consequences when we rebel against His direct orders.

In Numbers chapter 20, we read about how the Israelites angered Moses to the point where he became carelessly defiant in the promotion of self. God told Moses to speak to the rock so that water would come forth and reveal the glory of God. However, Moses responded in anger, struck the rock, and elevated himself in the process. Nonetheless, God allowed the water to come forth, not in support of Moses but to reveal His faithful and merciful ways. Unfortunately, Moses had to pay dearly for deviating from God's orders. He was not allowed to enter the "promised land." We see that Moses was out of order when he disobeyed God and promoted himself from being a representative of God, acting as though he and God were on the same level. As men of God, be mindful that the burdens of the people are not yours to bear alone, and you need not become overwhelmed by their demands or allow their frustrating and ungrateful ways to cause you to sin. As representatives of God, always look to God and lean on God so that He will enable you to lead with mercy, love, and integrity.

Called for a Higher Purpose

Today, most men have yet to realize or walk in the true calling and purpose that God has for them. As male ambassadors for Christ, it is important to realize that you are called to lead God's children back to Him. You are called to act as priests in your homes, and you are called to raise God-fearing children. This is a mammoth task that was never intended to be done alone or under mere human strength. Therefore, always be mindful that, with God's help, you can and will get the job done. As for spiritual things, which are often beyond our comprehension, God gave us His Holy Spirit to keep us in line with His will for our lives.

On the other hand, when it comes to dealing with the natural order of things, God has gifted you with women who are meant to complement you, help you, and walk beside you. Therefore, depending on God and working along with your companion is the only way to accomplish the will of the Lord. If this were not so, God would not have gifted us with His Holy Spirit, which is our divine Helper, and He would not have ordained the holy union between a man and a woman.

Serving vs. Being Served

It is critical for every Godly man to realize that his position of authority is an unmerited privilege. This means that a selfish, oppressive, haughty, or "laid back" attitude should never overshadow or contaminate such God-given authority. By being true to God, a man would unwaveringly serve others and inadvertently reap all the benefits worthy of a true king. Respect and loyalty are earned, and like Jesus pointed out in His teachings, he who desires to be great in the kingdom of God must first be a servant to others. Hence, a good leader strategizes and seeks to fulfill the needs of those who look up to him. As a direct result of providing for and protecting those who depend on him, he subsequently becomes the recipient of adoration and respect. On the other hand, a corrupt leader is often fickle or double-minded, seeks to be served by others, feigns interest in the needs of those who look up to him, and demands respect and loyalty in the face of oppression. Those who look up to him respond to this kind of leadership with mutiny and rebellion. As men of God, take time to engage in objective introspection to see what kind of leader you are, be it in your homes, in your church, on your job, or elsewhere. If you have fallen short in any way, make amends and purpose in your hearts that you will move forward with reformed attitudes and motives.

Spiritually Grounded and Confident

Also, be mindful that trying to intimidate and suppress a strong woman is a subconscious or deliberate act of oppression and insecurity. However, a strong woman is not to be confused with an obstinate or undermining female who undoubtedly may need to be "put in her place" occasionally. It is important to realize that your companion is comparable to you, and this means that God has gifted you with whatever it takes to match her strength. By faith, you should be able to recognize that a strong and intelligent mate is in direct correlation and proportion with how strong and intelligent you are. The only one who is asked to acquiesce in marital relationships is the woman because God has mandated that the man be the leader of the household and the church. Therefore, be merciful and try to understand that if the woman in your life has not yet realized that it takes strength to respect and yield to God-given authority, pray that the revelation comes to her sooner rather than later, all the while treating her as if she were a rare and most precious jewel.

However, you must always be careful never to compromise on any Godly standard or principle to please a woman. Furthermore, you should never let the women in your lives cause you to walk contrary to the will of God. Be wise and learn from the mistakes of biblical characters such as Adam, Samson, Solomon, David, and Ahab. These men all paid dearly for compromising on Godly principles because of the direct or indirect influence of the women in their lives. The weaknesses that were revealed in these leaders are not for you to emulate but for you to be aware of what happens when any man, including God's anointed, chooses to be led by the flesh rather than the Spirit, which is the Helper given to humankind.

I dare say, when it comes to some women and some situations that you may encounter in this life, you should hastily deflect to

Joseph mode (Genesis 39:1-20). Flee, because the safety of your soul literally depends on your narrow escape.

Remembering God's Purpose and Plan

It takes a man to lead in the home and in the church, not because he is a superior being, but simply because it was mandated by God for our own good. God, who is much wiser than any human being, chose man to be the head of the home and the head of the church. Therefore, He has gifted man with some unique qualities as well as the grace which allows him to carry out this mandate as long as he trusts in God. However, women were not given this mandate, so there are instances where she can imitate but never duplicate what God requires. Once males and females realize that we were both created in God's image to fulfill and carry out specific and distinct purposes in the kingdom of God, we would no longer have to act as though we are fighting for territorial rights. Furthermore, men would realize that it is poor taste and unacceptable to treat women as though they are inferior beings, instead of valued equals with differing roles.

As representatives of Christ, be mindful that Satan has been wreaking havoc on God's plan for our lives and has set in motion colossal confusion and numerous dysfunctional situations in this world. He has been the key distributor of the yeast that has adversely affected our lives. Ignorantly or willfully, we deflect to him by seeking and respecting the wisdom of "man" to help us remedy every situation. In an endless cycle of trial and error, we appease ourselves with temporary solutions that compound the situations further and ultimately lead to the search for more solutions. Are we so foolish to believe that the father of all lies, counterfeit, and deceit has the answers that will benefit humankind? Satan did not make us, does not understand us, does not want what is best for us, will never care for us, and will never do anything to ensure our victorious living. Hence, the mess we find ourselves in is a direct result of disobeying and rebelling against the commands and principles of God.

Our Heavenly Father has given us all that we need to experience abundant living here on earth and in the world to come. So, as leaders, remember that it takes you to stand up and carry out your God-given purpose. Many strong and capable women have been standing in the gap for a very long time, but as you can see, "a woman's touch" is not enough and will not suffice in God's system of decency and order. Remember how God accepted animal sacrifices temporarily until the blood of Jesus Christ was shed for our sins? In the same way, God will only use a woman to do so much. Therefore, as men of God, you must stop going with the flow, stop accepting what you know is contrary to the will of the Lord, and do what you have been called to do. Lead the people and take care of your families. 1 Timothy 5:8 states, "But if anyone does not provide for his own, especially for those of his household, he has denied the faith and is worse than an unbeliever."

Stepping Up to The Challenge

Considering that God's intended leaders (men) have already allowed a colossal mess to be perpetuated in the world, it will take nothing short of the power of God, which is the Holy Spirit working in you and through you, to rectify the situation. The world is changing, and many Godly principles are viewed as outdated, and the so-called "modern man" and the "modern family" are now commonplace. However, what the "world" does is no business of ours because we do not live by the world's standards. We adhere to God's standards and principles. Remember that Christians are followers of Christ, not worldly trends. Our standards should impact the world, so we should not sit back and allow the world to lead us astray. Do not be deceived by the seemingly sophisticated and overly tolerant ways of the world. The same God who abhorred sexual immorality and homosexuality in the Old Testament still considers them to be an abomination today. You cannot practice immoral and unclean lifestyles by biblical standards and expect to inherit eternal life. Jesus allowed His blood to be shed so that we can be washed clean from all unrighteousness. As born-again believers, you must constantly and consciously lay aside the "old man" and put on the holy character of Christ. 1 Thessalonians

4:7-8: "For God did not call us to uncleanness, but in holiness. Therefore, anyone who rejects this does not reject man, but God, who has also given us His Holy Spirit." So, stay focused on who you are as an ambassador for the kingdom of heaven and what you were called to do. You must do all that you can with God's help to lead the people back to God, not away from God!

As leaders in the house of God, engage in regular fasting and praying for the renewal of strength and inspiration to maintain law and order in the house of God and to lead God's flock into the light. As employers, fathers, and husbands, find ways to genuinely serve and effectively meet the needs of those who look up to you and depend on you. As husbands, go the extra mile to show how much you appreciate the support, opinion, and contribution of the women in your lives. As fathers, take the time to train and enjoy the children that God has blessed you with. Finally, as ambassadors for God, always remember that you are gifted with spiritual, emotional, intellectual, financial, and material abundance so that you can be a constant blessing to others. The realization of this truth leads to the continuity of abundant living on earth and the storing up of treasures in the world to come.

Remembering Your God-Given Purpose in The World

As men of God, always be mindful that God only wants you to be a willing and yielded instrument for the work of His Kingdom. From that point onward, He fights for you, with you, and through you every step of the way, as long as you continue to have faith in Him. If you find doing the work of the Lord anything less than enjoyable, fulfilling, and satisfying, this could mean that you are probably trying to "do something for the Lord" of your own accord, related to your own desires and in your human strength and ability. On the other hand, if you know without a shadow of a doubt that God has called you to do something and you still find it difficult, chances are, you may be "walking in the flesh" or "walking by sight." To have good success, take time to study, fast, pray, and renew your faith walk with God daily. Trust that there is nothing impossible or too hard for God to do. Remember that when

God calls you to do something, He always gives you the strength to endure and the grace to bring it to fruition.

As male ambassadors for Christ, I must admonish you that you must consistently put your faith and trust in God. Apart from God, there is no other source of deliverance, provision, and protection under the sun. It is unwise to sway back and forth between trusting in man's ability and the power of God. It is also important to ensure that you obey the commands and mandate of God to the letter. There is no room for deviation, alteration, or adaptations to God's words even if you have the best of intentions. Remember, God has graciously chosen to include and use you in carrying out a specific task. Therefore, show good sense and gratitude by leading and serving in a manner that brings glory and honor to God. The Bible gives the account in 1 Samuel 15 of how King Saul lost his anointing by not obeying a direct command despite his good intentions. He was admonished to heed the voice of the Lord, but he decided to do things his way. The Bible also documents in 2 Chronicles 15-16 how King Asa erred and failed by choosing to join forces with the enemy rather than turn to God, even though God had delivered, protected, and fought for him in the past. The book of 1 Kings 11 records how even Solomon, in all of his wisdom, failed God by following his wives and worshiping strange gods. These are just a few examples of good men who started out in right standing with God but failed as leaders because they did not obey God or trust Him wholeheartedly and constantly as they should have.

Staying Faithful to God

On the other hand, the Bible also bears a record of a king named Josiah (2 Kings 22-23) who had good success because he chose to honor God by restoring the house of worship and by redirecting adherence to the laws of God. It is said of King Josiah in 2 Kings 23:25, "Now before him there was no king like him, who turned to the Lord with all his heart, with all his soul and with all his might according to all the Law of Moses; nor after him did any arise like him." As ambassadors for Christ, let your record of leadership be one of continued good standing with our Heavenly Father, whether it is in your homes, on your jobs, in the church, in public office, or in some other leadership capacity. Remember to serve with integrity and labor to ensure that your actions and decisions bring glory to the Living God. Moreover, always strive to lead with love and compassion; know who you are, what is expected of you, and trust only in the wisdom and power of Almighty God as your source of provision, courage, and strength in all things and in every situation.

Regrettably, it is simply not enough for you to strive to live uprightly. You also have a solemn duty to instruct, guide, correct, admonish, and hold accountable all those who are under the protection of your name or your leadership. It seems to be the manner of some to think that everything will go well with them if they live upstanding lives and serve faithfully. There are also those who take a hands-off approach when it comes to dealing with the decisions and actions of their adult children. However, I think there is a very valuable lesson to be learned from the story of Eli and his two sons as recorded in 1 Samuel chapters 2 to 4. According to the scriptures, Eli was a priest of the Lord, and yet his sons were described as "sons of Belial" and not knowing the Lord.

Further, these sons were unfit for their duties and misused their positions. However, when Eli learned about the atrocious behavior of his sons, he spoke as if he had no authority or duty to uphold the standard in the Lord's house. Instead of removing his sons from their posts or relieving them of their duties, he left them to continue making a mockery of the things of God. Even though there was no mention of Eli himself willfully deviating from his duties as a priest, there is the blatant inference that he failed as a father and leader in the house of God. He did not raise God-fearing children, and he also did not check his sons when they strayed relative to the things of God. As a result, a curse was pronounced upon Eli, his sons, and his household. As I said earlier, men of God, you have a duty to sometimes take drastic measures to ensure that the word of God and the things of God are not compromised in any way to please anyone. Otherwise, be ready to accept the curses and hardships that will befall you and those you love when you put yourself before or above the will of God.

Men of vision, write your plan. Write it, pray over it, discuss it with God, and rework it often. You need a plan to lead effectively and to combat the varying situations that may arise in your homes, churches, communities, and workplaces. Your written plan will help you to execute your vision. Your vision is essential, because without it, all those who look up to you will perish for lack of good counsel and quality leadership. You must know your plan by heart, and you must not deviate from it to please any human being. If you don't have a plan and have no clue where to start, pray to God for help and search the scriptures to see what God expects you to do as a leader in whatever capacity you are placed in. Trust God in everything and for everything, never lean on your own understanding, and avoid counsel that is contrary to the will of God. There is no match for God when it comes to precise instructions and recommendations that will benefit you and those who look up to you.

Remember that God loves you, and He desires to see you have good success. So, be of good courage as God told Joshua (Joshua 1), because the Lord will always be with you as long as you teach and follow His commands and statutes. Commit to the ways of the Lord and be bold, decisive, and sincere like Joshua (Joshua 24:15), deciding that you and your household will serve the Lord, even when it is not popular. Be mindful, however, that if you stray from the will of God and still manage to deceive all humankind about your standing with God, it is God who searches the heart, knows all intent, and is aware of all your deeds. He is the ultimate Judge, and you must give an account of your stewardship to Him. So, do all that you can, all your days, in all your ways, to remain in right standing with God.

For more Scriptural study related to this chapter,

go to page 157.

CHAPTER 7

Virtuous Women

Embracing Humility and Modesty

Here is a perspective that has been made to seem so ridiculous, distasteful, outdated, and demeaning that most people deflect from it to the very detriment of our societies. 1 Peter 3:3-7 and 1 Timothy 2:9-13 teaches that women are to be modest in their apparel, behavior, and disposition. Women are also encouraged to submit to male authority and serve more supportive roles rather than leadership roles in church and their homes. Based on these Scriptures, the most outstanding and captivating thing a woman can do is let her true beauty and goodness shine from within. This means that focus is not merely on outward appearance and apparel or the pursuit of personal ambitions, but instead on the quality of one's relationships with and treatment of others. As a woman of God who respects the word of God as a divine manual for effective Christian living (2 Timothy 3:16-17), I believe that this is the model to pattern after, so that we can help with the critical development of our children to become God-fearing and positively productive human beings.

This model also enables us to reap many rewards on earth and the hope of receiving the promises of God in the world to come. I believe that the existing shift in roles and focus of females in society (often out of necessity) is a well-crafted distraction that has led to countless dysfunctional families as well as many neglected, severely misguided and underdeveloped children. Any fair-minded adult who reflects objectively would realize that families would be doing a much better job of replenishing the earth with a generation of God-fearing people, who have a high regard for human life and are more capable stewards of the world we live in, if men and women functioned more optimally in their God-given roles.

As female ambassadors for Christ, it is important to realize that we have a very crucial role to play in God's plan for humankind. We should never feel slighted or "less than" because of the things that we are called to do. As a matter of fact, it takes special strength and very unique qualities to be a virtuous woman. Furthermore, God is the one who made us, and He knew the exact purpose for His unique creation. After everything was created, the woman was like the missing piece of a puzzle, and therefore, she was created to fill a specific station. There are times when this "missing piece" may seemingly fit into other parts of the puzzle, but the fact remains; the woman is best suited for the role that she was created to fill.

Today, women have to try to substitute and serve in roles that were ultimately meant to be filled by men. However, in the decency and order of things, the "woman" was created to walk beside the "man" to support and be a helpmeet to him. As adults, we often must set rules and put boundaries in place for the benefit of those in our care. Likewise, our Heavenly Father has mandated a Godly system that is meant for our ultimate benefit. Nonetheless, we are all at liberty to do what pleases us and what seems right to us, but we must be mindful that anyone who defies or goes against the will of God is not a child of God and, therefore, will not have access to eternal life.

Respecting God-Ordained Assignments

As women of God, we should always allow God to deal with the individuals that He chooses to serve in a special capacity for Him. It is not our place to demote a servant of God, no matter how much we may think that they have "messed up," and no matter how much we feel as if we could do a much better job. Our duty is to know our roles well and function optimally in that capacity. There is a valuable lesson to be learned in Numbers 12. Moses was chosen by God to lead the children of Israel out of Egypt, and his sister Miriam had the privilege of sharing in this amazing opportunity by working alongside him. However, Miriam made the mistake of presuming that since Moses was a mere man and subject to certain faults, she could question his authority, undermine him, or act separately and apart from his authority. She was struck with leprosy, and the very same man whose calling she had questioned ended up having to pray for her healing. As women of God, we should always check our attitudes and our motives for doing things and always pray that God will deliver us from presumptuous sins. We need to realize that our lives, our husbands, and our families will all be better off if we follow the plan and purpose that God so wisely set out for us.

Today, we have embraced and accepted many characteristics as indicators of strength or independence, but they are all polluted with symptoms of weakness. Have you ever truly considered what qualities personify a weak person? A weak person asserts and shows off his or her power constantly. A weak person needs to be recognized and praised for everything he or she does. A weak person cannot and does not serve others well. A weak person thinks that serving is demeaning. A weak person seeks to satisfy his or her own needs at the expense of others. A weak person is not able to give without expecting something in return. A weak person is unable to love unconditionally. A weak person is insecure and reacts harshly to personal injustices. A weak person can never put the need of another before his or her own. A weak person has very little self-control in any situation. As women of God, we must realize and accept the fact that God's plan for our lives is far from submission as defined by the world, but rather it requires unique ability, great spiritual focus, and real strength.

Submitting for The Greater Good

We need to recognize that any behavior contrary to the will of God is an indication that we have not fully accepted or activated our mandate as true ambassadors for Christ. Over the years, I have learned to accept my personality and my character as a very strong woman. I am no damsel in distress. I am not submissive in every situation, and I believe that I can do almost anything just as good as, or even better than, most men. These are qualities that will remain true about me until the day I die. Yet, I consider myself to be a normal child of God. I am a strong woman, simply because I was made in the image of God. The fact that I am strong, made in the image of God, and a God-fearing woman, make it incumbent on me to acquiesce and follow God's plan for a woman in the church as well as in the home. To be honest, I know what it takes to lead. I am familiar with the demands that are placed on a leader, and I know what it is like to have people rely on me or look up to me for seemingly everything. However, I also have the good sense to step aside, show support, and allow a man of Godly vision to take the lead. I wholeheartedly believe that I can be of much greater benefit to my children and those around me if I served the role that would allow me to dot the "i's," cross the "t's," and fill in the gaps that a person who is busy leading would not have the time to do. Women of God, believe me when I say that so much goes unattended and neglected when we busy ourselves with leadership roles. I will never believe the world's system is more appealing than God's plan and purpose for His children. I have found that Godly choices and behavior always result in manifold blessings which include spiritual rest, peace of mind, and true contentment.

God's commands and statutes are not fashion or trends. They are immutable and unchangeable. As women of God, our standards for living are clearly set out in the Bible and will never change. We must also remember that God is and will never be outdated. He is God, and He does not need to change to "appeal to" anything or anyone. Instead, we are called to be holy just as our Father in Heaven is holy (1 Peter 1:16). This is a higher standard of living in Jesus Christ. Therefore, we should not give in to temptation or be swayed by the fleetingly attractive trends of the world, because rebellion and disobedience keep us outside the realm of holiness.

Furthermore, no matter how seemingly frustrating and clueless some men may be, it is never okay to engage in "male-bashing" or other behavior that emasculates the men around you. There is also no justifiable reason under the sun for any Godly woman to pursue an intimate relationship with another individual of the same sex. By biblical standards, it is unnatural, immoral, and unacceptable for two women (or two men for that matter) to engage in sexual acts, even under the farce of marriage sanctioned by humankind. Nonetheless, as with all things, I believe that we are all free to choose, to do as we please, and to follow whatever path makes us happy. However, every true woman of God knows that there is a Day of Reckoning and that some choices will lead to eternal life, while others will lead to eternal damnation.

Headstrong for Ages

Many of the contrary actions and ideas we display in our homes and sometimes in the workplace go all the way back to our tendency to undermine authority. This wayward behavior began thousands of years ago in the Garden of Eden when Eve chose to disobey God and dishonor her husband by listening to the Devil. She misused her influence over Adam and inadvertently led him astray. How many of you have objectively considered what might have happened if Eve had used her God-given influence for good and served her God-given purpose in the Garden? Furthermore, why would you pattern after biblical characters such as Delilah, Potiphar's wife, Jezebel, Queen Vashti, or Athaliah? The choices these women made undermined the men in their lives and did not honor God in any way. On the other hand, women like Sarah, Hannah, Esther, Deborah, Ruth, Mary, and Dorcas are examples of biblical characters who did not undermine the men in their lives, but rather served others and honored God with the choices that they made. As women of God, these are the kind of women that we should regard as timeless role models.

God's Word Stands Regardless of Appearances

After Adam and Eve's fall from grace, there were specific penalties for their disobedience to God. In Genesis 3:16, God said to Eve, "I will greatly multiply your sorrow and conception; in pain, you shall bring forth children; your desire shall be for your husband, and he shall rule over you." Many women disregard this portion of Scripture. When we rebel against that Scripture, we are making God's word of no consequence in our lives. Some say that the days when a man led his household are long gone because times have changed, right? Well, if the Creator is in favor of the changing roles of men and women, how is it that today's men are not born with ovaries or wombs? Better yet, explain why natural childbirth continues to be a great source of pain and discomfort as it was destined to be since Adam and Eve's eviction from the Garden of Eden. Humankind, in its wisdom, has tried to interfere and intervene by using artificial measures, but one should only be convinced that the words that God spoke in the Garden of Eden are null and void when every woman, regardless of her status, station, or belief can bring forth a child in this world "naturally" without experiencing any pain or discomfort. We should not be deceived into thinking that humankind's contrary behavior and so-called advancements can ever stand against the wisdom or the word of God.

As wise women of God, we should humbly endure all things with faith, hope, and love, looking forward to the full and true restoration that is ours in Christ Jesus. By doing what God requires of us, as with all things, we end up as the recipients of God's manifold blessings. We should note that God, in His matchless wisdom, works all things out for the good of His children. If we feel like we must stand up for ourselves and do so much for ourselves as women of God, then why do we need to serve the all-Powerful, God who promises to take care of us? A woman was never meant to take the place of a man. However, God can and will use a woman to bring the enlightenment of the gospel of grace to her family and anyone else with whom she gets the opportunity to interact through her ministry or service to others.

God's Plan vs. The Modern Woman

Today, it is quite normal for a woman to "run" things and excel at positions that were once dominated by males. It is accepted as common sense when a woman chooses a career and personal success rather than a husband and children. They are praised and admired for the time and attention they put into developing themselves professionally and physically. This is all good and well if our only purpose on earth was to pursue selfish ambitions, personal gratification, and success at the expense of the family. Today, women are rarely encouraged to become homemakers who support their husbands and help cultivate the minds of children to grow up and become a positive influence in the world. As a matter of fact, the virtuous woman that is praised and to be desired in Proverbs 31:10-31 is now looked upon with disdain.

To make matters worse, some women view children as an inconvenience, a commodity, a burden, or a liability rather than a blessing from God. Such widespread deception and self-serving behavior and mindsets have undoubtedly been perpetuated by Satan. Who else would want to keep God's children from realizing and fulfilling their true purpose on the earth?

Women of God, we should never act as if God owes us something or cannot do anything without our help. Instead, we should be grateful to God for including us in His redemption plan. It is mercy and grace that has afforded us the opportunities that we have in the kingdom. Therefore, a wise woman would act out of humility and dedication to ensure that the will of the Lord is done where and whenever she has the opportunity. Our main goal should be to deliberately and consciously operate in the strength of God and submit to God-appointed authority. Meanwhile, we also need to be mindful that if our husbands and the other male figures in our lives have not yet come to the light (which is the recognition and actualization that they are accountable for the proper leadership and ultimate welfare of their families and the church), we can take our situation to God in prayer and trust God to set things in order.

Being A Real Help Meet

As strong women of God, it is in our best interest to do all that we can to ensure that the men in our lives become more aware of their God-given status on this earth. Does this mean that we should be or end up as servants and slaves to the men in our lives?

Certainly, not! Contrary to the major and popular deception, serving or slaving for the men in our lives is not and never was God's intention for any woman. God told Eve that her husband would rule over her, but he never said that she would be a slave or servant to him. A ruler is someone in a position of authority over others. The rulers of the world are often corrupt, misguided, and selfish in many ways. This is very unappealing for any woman who considers being under the rulership of her husband fated with such distasteful circumstances. However, men who are influenced by God act as servants of the people. They are generous and just, and they show compassion for their subjects. Therefore, a woman of God can rest easy, knowing that she will always be appreciated, protected by, and provided for by her Godly husband.

When we, as female believers, help the men in our lives to become more aware of and accept their God-given status as kings in their homes, we automatically become the companions of kings. The complementary companion of a king on the earth is a queen. It is part of God's plan for men and women to rule together as kings and queens over their own households. It is desirable for women of God to "be wise as serpents and gentle as doves" (Matthew 10:16). If we truly want to please God, we simply need to relinquish the stolen spotlight, and our desires will soon become our reality by simple association. The following saying has real merit in the Godly system of things; "behind every good or successful man is a strong and supportive woman."

As true women of God, we need to realize that God made man and woman with unique and distinct characteristics, two separate parts of one whole. Therefore, a comparable companion is likeminded in many ways but complements you in all the ways that matter in God's kingdom. What does this mean? This means that it is good to marry someone who is diversely abled, and we should never try to get our companions to be replicas of ourselves or fuss at them about their ways. We should be careful not to quickly pass the blame, deny responsibility, or throw in the towel before we subject ourselves to a thorough and objective spiritual introspection. Many of the problems we face in our marital relationships are a direct result of trying to fix "spiritual problems" by consulting and adhering to the "wisdom and principles of man."

God's Way is Best

God has ordained marriage; the union between a man and a woman. Are we so jaded and reckless to believe that He did not give us the manual on how to gain maximum benefits from such a union? As with all good things that God has gifted us with, He gave us the Bible as a manual to ensure the utmost benefits and ultimate satisfaction. However, if we forget our Maker and try to fix our problems by using alternative measures, we will not get much satisfaction or ultimate benefits from our marital relationships. Just remember that Satan is on a mission to kill, steal, and destroy all of God's blessings which are intended for our joy-filled living. Therefore, if we experience disappointments or problems in our marriages, the key is to go to God and ask Him to help us fix the mess that we have created through the choices we have made. Many of us have taken away God's pleasure and opportunity of providing for us and working for us by trying to solve our own problems or by giving up on potentially good relationships. Most of the problems we face in our relationships can be worked out if we remember and try to live by these basic principles: love one another as we love ourselves and treat others the way that we would like or expect to be treated.

As virtuous women of God, if for any moment we are assailed by doubt and unbelief that it is indeed God's will for males to lead the Church as well as their households (especially when many men seem to be incapable of doing so according to our critical eyes), remember the Israelites whom Moses led out of Egypt. God instructed them and provided for them, yet they disobeyed Him, rebelled against Him, and did not have the faith to see where God was taking them. Therefore, all the unbelievers died in the wilderness and were never allowed to enter the promised land. I say, let us live to enjoy the promised land in our marriages by using biblical principles as the recipe and guide for the things we practice in our households. As truly enlightened believers, let us rest in Jesus, trust His system of things, and not risk losing our souls through our good intentions or blatant defiance. By resting in Jesus, we would please Him with our lifestyles and be a light to those who are still burdened with the cares and standards of the world. Furthermore, remember that the key to a truly purpose-filled life, successful marriage, and abundant living is to trust God and adhere to His standard of living.

For more Scriptural study related to this chapter, go to page 157.

CHAPTER 8

"Suffer the Little Children to Come unto Me"

Our Duty as Christian Parents

"My people are destroyed for lack of knowledge, because you have rejected knowledge, I will also reject you from being priest for Me; because you have forgotten the law of your God, I will also forget your children" (Hosea 4:6).

As Christian parents, it is high time we realize that we will perish, future generations will self-destruct, and the very souls of our children are at stake unless we show them the way that they should go. We must teach our children about God and train them well in the ways of God. Children are never too young to learn about God and biblical principles. If we educate them about God and teach them what God expects from His creation, they will have a good foundation to build their lives upon. It is this training that provides a haven of rest and to which children can deflect in moments of temptation, when doubt arises, or when peer pressure demands deviant behavior. Outside of Christ, there is no real hope for future generations. A generation without Christ, biblical principles, and Godly values can only self-destruct. The only hope for a brighter tomorrow will be because of those individuals who make it their life's mission to perpetuate the will of God on the earth by nurturing God-fearing seed even when holding fast to certain beliefs and values seems "taboo" in the eyes of so many. We ultimately know that the acknowledgment of God and adherence to God's will is the "knowledge" that saves us from destruction. Psalm 111:10:

"The fear of the Lord is the beginning of wisdom; A good understanding have all those who do His commandments."

In Matthew 19:14, Jesus says, "Let the little children come to Me, and do not forbid them; for such is the kingdom of heaven." This is no indication that we should indulge our children in their folly, but rather we should strive to nurture their good qualities and teach our children about their Lord and Savior at a tender age. Children are very pliable during their formative years. Therefore, it makes sense to instill Godly standards and principles in them so that they would always have the best foundation upon which to build the rest of their lives.

Another reason why parents should adhere to Jesus' words in Matthew 19:14 is because young children will one day become adults with their own children and the responsibility of raising the next generation of God-fearing people. If we fail to teach the relevant and crucial things to our children, the principles of Godly living, as well as regard for Christ, will die with us. When we read the Old Testament, there are many accounts of how the children of God strayed and suffered many misfortunes because they forgot God and followed the ways of the people around them.

As God-fearing parents, we must always be mindful that God has entrusted us with a very critical responsibility. If we fail to teach our children about God or Jesus Christ, they will grow up to become a lawless generation. They will become a callous generation whose imaginations will abound in the opposite extreme. 2 Timothy 3:1-5 admonishes, "But know this, that in the last days, perilous times will come: for men will be lovers of themselves, lovers of money, boasters, proud, blasphemers, disobedient to parents, unthankful, unholy, unloving, unforgiving, slanderers, without self-control, brutal, despisers of good, traitors, headstrong, haughty, lovers of pleasure rather than lovers of God, having a form of godliness but denying its power. And from such people turn away." As Christian parents, do you think we should be so clueless, overindulgent, and reckless in the rearing of our children that we become the vehicles that allow this prophecy to come to pass on our watch? The next question is this: do you believe that this passage is referring to the children that would have been brought up to fear and show high regard for God and the principles of God? I think not. That is why Jesus says suffer the little children to come unto Him because He knows that in Him is a better way of life and a much more promising future for our children.

Misguided Parenting

As adults, we are very keen to shield and shelter children from what we think will hurt them, so we often lapse into folly that is seemingly harmless. Christian parents should never revert to the perpetuation of fairytales or characters such as the Tooth Fairy, Santa Claus, and the Easter Bunny at the expense of the things of God. Why make up characters for your children to believe in while downplaying the reality of Almighty God and our Savior Jesus Christ? We think it was ridiculous that people in biblical times could create images and worship them in the face of The Living God even after experiencing and witnessing countless miracles at the hand of Almighty God. Well, how hypocritical are we if we spend time feeding our children fairy tales rather than teaching them about our Heavenly Father? During the most critical and formative years of our children's lives, we spend valuable time helping to perpetuate the existence of made-up characters, but we apply little or no effort to teaching our children about God and the things of God.

Children need their parents to teach them how to become God-fearing individuals. Without that valuable input into our children's lives, we fail as parents, no matter what else we provide and no matter how dedicated and consistent we may be at providing those other things. If you introduce made-up characters into your children's lives for whatever reason, be careful to teach your children the difference between reality and fantasy. Furthermore, you should always make a deliberate and consistent effort to teach your children that God is very real, even though we cannot see or touch Him. In addition, teach them that God is our creator, we are made in His image, and there is evidence of His existence all around us.

Is the idea of God so farfetched that we need to create make-believe characters to fill a void that only the Creator is meant to fill? We misinterpret what it means to love our children. Instead of being God-fearing parents or guides who help to channel our children's enthusiasm, interests, and fantasies into meaningful endeavors, many times, we overindulge them and allow them to excessively engage in self-serving behaviors. However, we must be ever mindful that children have great perceptions and an ability to accept things that many adults have become too jaded to accept. I understand the idea of wanting to create tangible and visible characters that children can identify with, but teaching children about God is even simpler and much more beneficial. Children can appreciate and accept things that adults with all their wisdom, acquired intelligence, and crippling logic may find difficult to accept. That is why Jesus wants us to become as little children as it relates to our faith.

Valuing the Formative Years

Children are born with some pure qualities such as trust, the ability to forgive and forget, concern for others, and the ability to believe in the impossible. These qualities should be encouraged, nurtured, and channeled at a very early age to curb the development of undesirable behavior, which seems to flourish with little or no encouragement. Children all around the world know how to play, use their imaginations, and get up to mischief. Therefore, instead of overindulgence in free play, we need to ensure that children receive some guidance and supervision to ensure that play involves experiences that positively impact real-life relationships.

As I alluded to earlier, children have very active imaginations, lots of unbridled energy, and very selfish natures. There are major risks as it relates to a child's spiritual, emotional, and physical well-being when these go unchecked and unchanneled. Nonetheless, with proper guidance and support, children can know true success when we teach them to put God first and have high regard for others. When parents have a desire for their children to grow up to make wise decisions and become truly successful, they should do all that is humanly possible to ensure that these children develop a relationship with the Creator from a very early age. As a matter of fact, it should go without saying; Christian parents raise Christian children. In a Christian household, children should not have a choice when it comes to believing in and serving Almighty God.

Children are a blessing, our legacy, and the opportunity for us to please Almighty God by helping to replenish the earth with a people who fear God and live by Godly principles. Therefore, it is important for us to teach our children about the living God. We must teach them to adhere to biblical principles such as respecting their elders, doing good, and shunning evil. We need to teach them the importance of being obedient and about the snare of rebellion. We need to demonstrate and teach values like selflessness and caring for others. We need to teach our children the difference between ambitions that are self-serving as opposed to endeavors that benefit others. As God-fearing parents, we also need to teach our children how to pray and how to study the Bible as a practical source of answers to life's many questions. We need to encourage our children to trust in the power of Almighty God to protect them, provide for them, and to heal them. If we can indulge their fantasies by allowing them to have superheroes that can do nothing for them, why is it so hard for us to take the time to teach them about the Creator of Heaven and Earth and the Sustainer of the universe? We do not need to fabricate a story about the existence of our Heavenly Father, because there is evidence of His existence all around us. Without the excellent handiwork of Almighty God, we would not know true love or real beauty, and we would have no natural resources from which all man-made things derive. Frankly, without God, we would not have our families to love and care for us or to share with.

As godly parents who know how awesome God is and how He does all things well, we should never underestimate our children's ability to understand and accept the things of God. We must give them a chance to get to know their Creator as well as their Lord and Savior. We cannot allow our children to live empty, worthless lives, void of common decency. We must steer them away from self-centeredness, selfish desires, and self-serving ways. As Christian parents, we need to give our children every opportunity to develop their spirit man. It is our duty to teach our children the virtue and value of sincere and appropriate prayer. We must afford our children the opportunity to experience and come to know genuine love, friendship, appreciation, and acceptance. This would curb the tendency to seek the fulfillment of these needs in unsavory places, from unsavory characters, and by unsavory means.

Instilling Godly Principles and Values

If we do not suffer the little children to come to Christ and get to know their Lord and Savior while they are young, is it any wonder that many of our children grow up with cold hearts, fickle identities, and no regard for Almighty God? We must lay aside our busyness and invest some real quality time in our children. This means applying consistent, loving, and thoughtful effort to teaching and disciplining our children. If we do not deliberately intervene, can we truly blame the children when they grow up to become vain, disrespectful, unloving, unconcerned, ungrateful, rebellious, void of godly principles, corrupt, full of evil intent, full of worldly lusts, ignorant of their Savior, unforgiving, and treacherous to all forms of life?

Let us learn from the biblical accounts of the Israelites in the Old Testament. There were years of peace, provision, and protection for Israel while the generations that observed God were alive. However, they neglected to teach their children about God and the goodness of God. So, the children disregarded godly standards and adopted the ways and the wisdom of those around them. Everyone did what was right in his/her own eyes. As children of the family and the age of grace, we have the opportunity and privilege of being called the Children of God, not through any merit of our own. Nonetheless, we are called to a higher standard of living in Jesus Christ. Therefore, we may "serve God" all our days, but we are doing a disservice to our children when we do not teach them to honor and value the things of God. As Christian parents, it should always be indisputable that you and those who dwell in your house serve God and strive daily to do the will of the Lord. Serving God should never be just an option in your homes, and there should be no tolerance for any type of behavior that goes against this fact. Parents should consider themselves to be truly successful parents only if they did all they could to instill godly principles and values in their children and helped them to come to the acceptance of Jesus Christ as their Lord and Savior. This is so because, even if these children stray, they will always remember the foundation upon which their lives were built, and they will return.

As parents, we do not have to force anything on our children, but we do pass on traditions and family values either by implicit and explicit instruction or simply by association. For example, most adults can attest to family vacations, Thanksgiving or Christmas dinners, and other family leisure moments. These traditions and memories are often continued for generations. Some are improved upon, and some may be discontinued for one reason or another. Nonetheless, the passing on of various traditions depends largely on the level of conviction, love, and enjoyment that children experience and observe in their parents or other adults around them. I believe that whatever is done lovingly, diligently, and consistently becomes a habit or a treasured part of one's life. It is often said that old habits are hard to break. So why not put deliberate effort into cultivating Godly habits, values, and traditions in our children? All the while, we must be careful to ensure that such cultivation occurs in a manner that is natural, meaningful, beneficial, essential, and perpetually relevant to the overall well-being of our families. We never want to impress upon our children that what we do is disconnected, meaningless, or cumbersome, thus prompting them to discontinue the important values and principles which lead to abundant living and keeps us in right standing with God.

Godly and Practical Love for Our Children

As Christian parents, we must answer our children's questions, value their ideas, channel their energy, and give them a purpose and reason for being. We should also regard them as valuable, a second chance to make it right with God, and a priceless legacy. When it comes to our little ones, we need to take the time to calm them and quiet their fears, not by creating fairy tales or by overindulgence. Instead, we should always provide biblical examples, Godly instruction, and opportunities for them to engage in selfless and altruistic activities. Children need rules, order, training, and guidance, as well as some tough love from time to time. This will help them to learn that there are consequences for certain choices or actions. Children are creative, imaginative, and even very insightful at times, and they thrive with our support. However, they still need structure with reasonable boundaries that will allow them to become productive, selfless, God-fearing adults.

Children are never meant to become our idols. They are not to be revered, worshiped, or over-celebrated, but they must always be viewed as an incredible responsibility. They are meant to be loved and trained to follow and live by Godly principles. As children of God, we know that our Heavenly Father chastens those whom He loves. Therefore, God-fearing parents who love their children would never let them grow wild and unfettered. God-fearing parents understand the need for discipline and boundaries. Contrary to the belief of those who rely on their own wisdom, children who are disciplined within the context of genuine love and concern never have repercussions like those who experience abuse at the hands of cruel, clueless, or misguided adults.

Train your children to be law-abiding citizens, full of integrity and common decency, with God as the nucleus of everything. As a people, we must know that all our efforts are purposeless if we concentrate solely on satisfaction and success in the "here and now." We must also prepare for the future of our souls. Most of us do not hesitate to plan for our futures in this world, as unknown as they are; we plan for retirement and college years, but we act as if we have no control over where we and our seed will spend eternity. However, there are so many successful individuals in the world who seemingly have everything their hearts could desire, but many would admit to having had a major void in their lives that could not be filled until their "spirit man" became attuned to the Holy Spirit. This is a testament that we need to help our children to develop not only as human beings but also as spiritual beings in tune with our heavenly Father, who is a Spirit.

We claim to love our children; so many of us go above and beyond to educate them and to provide for them physically. We are also so tolerant, accepting, and appeasing that we supposedly help with emotional, psychological, and social adjustments. Essentially, we teach our children to fit into the world as we know it. However, as Christians, neither our children nor we are supposed to fit into the world. Instead, we are meant to transform the world for the better by raising Godly seed. Furthermore, we do very little to help save the souls of our children, and we do very little to deliberately nurture them as spiritual beings who need to be in constant communion with our Spiritual Father, who is in Heaven. We claim to love our children so much, but we hardly spend any time thinking about investing in their souls, the part of them that will live forever.

Peculiar Parenting

Modern parents do not spend time thinking about or investing in the "real" future of their children. However, as children of God, we should not be ashamed to let the world know that we care about the souls of our children. Saying that out loud even sounds a bit "looney," but that is okay. Why claim to believe in God and the gift of salvation through His Son Jesus Christ if we are ashamed to accept all the responsibility that comes with such knowledge and association? Proverbs 26:18: "Where there is no revelation, people cast off restraint. But happy is he who keeps the law." As Christian parents, we need to accept the vision that God has for His children and live by the principles that ensure lasting contentment.

Our ways may seem peculiar or even crazy in the eyes of many of those around us who have become consumed with worldly wisdom, but in the end, we all must give an account for our lives and our legacy. Your legacy is your children. When you give an account of what you did to ensure that you left behind a Godly legacy, let it be a testament of your efforts to instill Godly values, principles, and habits in your children. If, for some reason, the children stray, let it not be because of you. You are responsible for every child that comes forth from you as well as those for whom you have chosen to nurture. When it comes to those in your household, make sure that they are aware of your

Godly standards and never compromise on those standards, even when they seem too strict or harsh to outsiders. Always be mindful that you can never love your children as much as our Heavenly Father, so trust God and the Bible as the guide to help you raise God-fearing children.

When I think about my children and what I hope they become as adults, to be honest, getting a good job or having a successful career is secondary in my book. As a woman of God, my proudest moment as a mother will be when I can witness my sons using free will to exemplify sincere appreciation and respect for the things of God and demonstrating genuine concern and consideration for others. I know with all my heart that these qualities will make them stand out and have good success wherever they go. In my book, success by the world's standards is okay, but to raise God-fearing and God-conscious children is the only way that we can help to save future generations from self-destructing.

When we think about the context in which Jesus used the words "suffer, the little children to come unto me" (Mark 10:14-15), the parents brought their children to Jesus to be touched and blessed by Him. So why do the parents of this generation leave the spiritual welfare of their children up to chance? Why do we get lulled into thinking that good parents need only provide food, clothes, shelter, smothering love, healthcare, education, and a personal cheering section for our children? Some of us go overboard by giving our children everything their little clueless hearts may desire. There is a serious problem with this approach to raising children. In most cases, the blatant outcome is that we only succeed at spoiling our children and making them feel entitled rather than privileged. Hence, we are the facilitators of an ungrateful, irreverent, and disrespectful generation. Proverbs 30:11-12 states, "There is a generation that curses its father, and does not bless its mother. There is a generation that is pure in its own eyes, yet is not washed from its filthiness." Remember, in all things and in every situation, you will reap what you sow. Also, be mindful that outside of Christ, even our best efforts are tainted with and ultimately leads to corruption.

"Suffer the Little Children to Come unto Me"

Biblical Standards for Disciplining Our Children

When you think of disciplining or punishing a child in any way for whatever reason, does the face or image of an obedient, innocent, cooperative, or angelic child pop into your mind? Hardly ever! This is because discipline or punishment is reserved for children who are usually willfully defiant, constantly exhibiting naughty behavior, or repeatedly engaging in actions that are dangerous or harmful to themselves and sometimes others. Therefore, the purpose of discipline or punishment, in this case, is not to abuse the child but rather to reform the child and, ultimately, to deter or permanently eradicate such behavior. With that said, I believe that some measures of discipline or punishment are more effective than others.

As Christian parents, we must always be mindful that biblical principles and instruction are for our ultimate benefit. So even when they seem harsh or outdated by the world's standards, Godly parents will hold fast to the words in 2 Timothy 3:16, "All Scripture is given by inspiration of God, and is profitable for doctrine, for reproof, for correction, for instruction in righteousness, that the man of God may be thoroughly equipped for every good work." Therefore, as Christian parents, we need not be afraid to chastise or discipline our children out of Godly love. It is our duty to "train up a child in the way he should go, and when he is old he will not depart from it" (Proverbs 22:6). If you set clear guidelines, rewards, or consequences and live by those consistently, children will become aware of acceptable and appropriate as well as inappropriate behavior.

However, I must say that if spanking is used as a deterrent to unacceptable or undesired behavior, it should always be administered after a briefing or discussion of what took place and should never be done harshly, in haste, in anger, or out of frustration. For many of us, a spanking is out of the question because it seems cruel and some would even say that it is barbaric in nature. However, I do not think that it is possible for any self-controlled and loving parent to administer a spanking that would ever be so extreme. Furthermore, we should never feel as though our children are too innocent or too precious to occasionally merit a spanking, especially the ones who seem totally void of a mild-mannered disposition. Therefore, we need to think of spanking as a "means to" the desired end, so there would eventually be no need for it. Proverbs 29:15 & 17: "The rod and rebuke give wisdom, but a child left to himself brings shame to his mother." "Correct your son and he will give you rest; yes, he will give delight to your soul." Proverbs 22:15: "Foolishness is bound up in the heart of a child; The rod of correction will drive it far from him." Proverbs 23:13-14: "Do not withhold correction from a child, for if you beat him with a rod he will not die. You shall beat him with a rod and deliver his soul from hell." I know many parents who wince at the words in those scriptures and cringe at the thought of laying a finger on their precious children. As a result, many have rejected those Scriptures over the years in favor of so-called progressive forms of discipline. Consequently, I believe that we are inadvertently creating this selfish, coldhearted, reckless, and morally deficient generation because we choose to willfully ignore or disregard the wisdom of the Bible in favor of flawed human logic.

Teaching Important Christian Cornerstones

"Suffer the little children to come unto me" also means that we should not hide the real reason we observe Good Friday or commemorate the Easter season. As a matter of fact, we make a mockery of Christ when we as Christians allow things like the Easter Bunny, Easter baskets, and Easter eggs to overshadow the story of Jesus' sacrifice, which is the only thing able to cleanse us from our sins. As Christians, we do not need to sit idly by and allow seemingly harmless things to take up our time and fill such large areas of our lives. We have a duty to dispel and downplay any myth that tries to detract from God or the things of God. The Easter Bunny and Easter Eggs, as well as Santa Claus, Christmas trees, and flying reindeer are distracting components of two holidays that are meant to bring honor, glory, and recognition to God and the orchestration of the amazing gift of salvation, but instead, we get caught up in made-up or meaningless traditions that only produce temporary feelings of goodwill. As Christian parents, our first duty is to teach our children about meaningful traditions and customs rather than try to keep up with worldly trends that are fleeting and temporarily satisfying. Pay attention, people; many of the things we do are not as harmless as we allow ourselves to believe, because anything we do at the expense of helping our children to become deeply rooted in Christ is a step towards our own ultimate doom. Proverbs 14:12: "There is a way that seems right to a man, but its end is the way of death."

Do not be afraid to tell your children about Jesus' sacrifice on Good Friday and His awesome resurrection on Easter Sunday. They should know that Jesus loves us so much that He "allowed" Himself to be punished for our sins. There is no reason to be sad because He did it willingly, and besides, He arose so that all who believe in Him may be washed clean by His blood and eventually live with Him forever.

Furthermore, the festivities of Christmas should revolve around the birth of Jesus Christ; whether the date is accurate or not is irrelevant. The important thing is that the words of John 3:16 should be the real message of the Christmas season. So, in gratitude for such an amazing gift, we should strive to be a blessing to others. Therefore, instead of focusing merely on the exchange of gifts between loved ones who are rarely "in need" in the first place, we should use this season to teach our children the importance of making something good happen in the life of someone less fortunate.

I love Christmas! It is my favorite time of the year. I just love the cheerful atmosphere and the feelings of goodwill that are more obvious around that time of year. However, over the years, I have watched the festivities grow and shift in focus so much so that Jesus is often left out, usually an afterthought or just a sideshow. This saddens me a great deal. I cringe at the day and the possibility when future generations will know nothing about the Nativity and the relationship between Christ and the season. As Christians, let us endeavor to keep the Christ in Christmas and His birth as the real reason for our celebrations by making more room for Him and placing special emphasis on these facts for the benefit of our children. Remember, "peace on earth and goodwill to men" only became a definite possibility due to the birth of the Christ child more than two thousand years ago. Therefore, let's continue to make a deliberate effort to instill this vision in the hearts and minds of our little ones so that they can grow with true insight as to how to make the world a significantly better place.

Perpetuating Truth vs. Fairytales

As Christian parents, we must be careful about the things we bring into our children's lives, no matter how innocent or popular they may be by worldly standards. As adults who should know better, why do we permit certain hypocrisies and go with the flow like the people in the story titled, "The Emperor's New Clothes?" We know that certain things are not right, but instead of speaking up and standing up for what is right, we go with the flow. In that story, everyone was afraid to speak up and say that the emperor was naked; it took a child to speak up. Children can handle plain and simple truths. Furthermore, they do not always need pictures and a story to get the truth either. Do you know that as adults, we tend to complicate the truth by fabricating stories that distort the truth and ultimately do nothing but make the truth itself look like a fairytale? It is better to teach your children the truth from a young age, especially as the need arises or when the opportunities present themselves. I believe this is best because, in most cases, children are more resilient when they are younger and tend to adjust and adapt more readily. However, it becomes another matter when we suddenly have to introduce truths to adolescents or teenagers after they have become accustomed to believing the fairytales for so many years.

In Biblical times, kings made decrees and proclamations that, if not followed, were punishable by death, such as in the book of Daniel, where we read about the three Hebrew boys and Daniel in the lion's den. However, these individuals stood up for what is right, even when faced with losing their lives. Nonetheless, in today's society, where most people have the freedom to speak up for their cause without penalty of death, Christians go along with almost everything. How can we lead the world or have any impact on the world if we allow people who have no regard for God or the things of God to dictate the way we live? Furthermore, if you share fairytales with your children, be sure to teach your children that those tales are make-believe and merely for entertainment, unlike Our Heavenly Father, the sustainer of the universe who created us and the world we live in. Telling the truth is not harsh! As a matter of fact, Christian parents need to be more adamant about raising God-fearing children as well as with their expectations of those who look to them for provision, protection, and guidance. It is poor taste for Christian parents to think that being "cool" or their children's friend is more important than being a guide and a source of real inspiration when it comes to Godly living. When we teach our children the truth about God, we spare them future heartache and disappointments. We also save them from their selfish nature when we teach them to deny themselves and embrace Jesus as their Savior.

Suffer Your Children to Come to Christ

I have heard it said, and I have heard it sung, so many times and in so many ways; "heal the world," "I believe the children are the future," "what the world needs is love," and so on. Undoubtedly, those words are sincere, on point, and very relevant to our times. However, the world will remain on the path to destruction, and the future will continue to have a bleak outlook if we do not come to our senses quickly. As Christians and God's well-loved creation, our sole purpose is to serve God and keep His commandments in return for abundant living and eternal life. Therefore, we must endeavor to perpetuate in all our generations a people who are God-conscious as well as a people who adhere to and have a reverence for the principles of God. This can only happen when we lay aside our personal will so that God's will can be done.

We must bring our children to Jesus for Him to bless them, instruct them, and give them their true purpose for living. We do this by teaching our children at a very early age who we are in Christ, why we were created, and what is expected of us as children of God. If we do not get weary in well-doing, our children will indeed grow up to be good stewards of the world, who trust God instead of leaning on their own understanding and their interpretation of the way things are or should be. Furthermore, even if we do not succeed in all cases, or even when it may seem as though we are fighting a losing battle with our teenagers, we must remain steadfast in our efforts and trust in God because He cannot lie (Numbers 23:19). According to Isaiah 55:11, "So shall My word be that goes forth out of my mouth: it shall not return unto me void, but it shall accomplish that which I please, and it shall prosper in the thing whereto I sent it." Therefore, it is the duty of the Christian parent to believe and fulfill Proverbs 22:6, which says, "Train up a child in the way he should go; and when he is old he will not depart from it." Ultimately, the only way that we can preserve our souls, save the world, and provide hope for future generations is to "suffer the little children" to come to the knowledge and saving power of the Lord Jesus Christ.

CHAPTER 9

Basking in Jesus

Good Will Triumph Over Evil

I love movies with happy endings, and I especially enjoy movies where *good* triumphs over *evil*. I always feel satisfied when, even after a most severe beat down, the superhero emerges victorious in the end. The reality is, we live in a world where evil is very prevalent, and the bad guys are usually the ones who always seem to be having a good day. This is not to say that there is no good present in our world, but it often seems to be no match for all the wickedness that is being perpetrated around us. Frankly, darkness seems to be casting a shadow over everything, and light appears to be rather scarce.

Nonetheless, I have hope, and I am excited! I believe in the power of God, and I know that evil and darkness will never win the final battle against goodness and light. As children of God, we cannot allow ourselves to be fooled by appearances. We cannot give up on goodness and our high standards for living just because it seems as if these qualities are no longer relevant or that "bad" is now the new good. Be ever mindful that no matter how prevalent corruption may be among the "worldly minded," corruption and all other forms of wickedness will come to an end! Stay true to God and keep your eyes on Jesus! Jesus has already won the victory! So, no matter how much destruction Satan may cause, Jesus is the real Super Man! He is the Savior of the world. He will ultimately destroy evil and do away with darkness forever. Stay tuned in to and rest in Jesus, because He is God's gift to us, enabling us to obtain true rest, incomparable peace, abundant life now, and eternal life in the world to come. Outside of Christ, there is no other way, power, person, place, animal, or thing that can save us, give us eternal life, or usher us into the presence of God.

Boosting Our Spiritual Immune System

1 Timothy 2:5-6 states that "there is one God and one mediator between God and men; the Man Christ Jesus, who gave Himself a ransom for all, to be testified in due time." For this reason, every true believer should rest in Jesus and trust that He is the only acceptable foundation for humankind's redemption back to God. God has the antidote for whatever ails His children, and we must go to Him willingly and trust Him to heal us totally and restore us to maximal functionality. Once He cleanses us of the infected yeast, which is Satan's ideas and deceit, He then gives us His Holy Spirit, which immunizes us against further and similar attacks on our spiritual immune system. As true believers, we should make certain through daily prayer, meditation, and the study of God's word that the dosage of our immunization (which is the Holy Spirit working in us and through us) is always at an optimal level; otherwise, we will constantly suffer from relapses.

Jesus reminded us in Luke 4:4 that "man should not live by bread alone, but by every word of God." The word of God, therefore, is the spiritual diet that we must feast on daily because even if we end up without physical food, the word of God is enough to sustain us. A nourished believer will be able to recognize the "hand" and the plans of Satan in even the most seemingly insignificant things. We know that we do not wrestle against flesh and blood (Ephesians 6:12), so it means that instead of going about ready to attack others, we would be spiritually aware of the enemy's hand in even the subtle things. Remember how Jesus responded to the temptations of Satan in the wilderness? In a natural state, Jesus would have been well-justified in yielding to each of the temptations that Satan brought before Him. However, Jesus' responses to the temptations accounted in Matthew 4:1-11 continue to be an example for us to follow every day.

Empowered by The Word

Let's take a few moments to reflect on the manner that Jesus was tempted (Matthew 4:1-11; Luke 4: 1-13). Based on these Scriptures, Jesus had just finished fasting and depriving His body of physical nourishment. So, He was starved. Therefore, as the powerful Son of God, when the idea came to Him to turn stones into bread, He could have had a meal in a heartbeat. However, He was so filled with spiritual food that His immediate response was a reply from God's word—not a word that would benefit Him and justify why He deserved some physical nourishment, but a word that brought ultimate glory to God. He simply stated that "man shall not live by bread alone, but by every word of God." When we put God first, above all things, have no doubt that God will indeed take care of our physical needs.

In the natural sense, Jesus would have also been justified in yielding to the second temptation that Satan brought to Him. After all, Jesus was about to begin His ministry on the earth, and having some material wealth and earthly connections would have aided His cause significantly, right? So, He could have justified why it was necessary to deviate from God's plan, which required humility and personal sacrifice, since He found a seemingly easier or better way to carry out His mission. However, Jesus was so filled with spiritual food that He recognized the snare of the enemy right away. Hence, he did not bow or yield to Satan, despite Satan presenting Him with a convenient counterfeit plan of power and kingdom rule. Further, Jesus was so spiritually alert that He could not be deceived into thinking that Satan actually had something to offer Him. So, instead of debating with Satan or even entertaining the idea, Jesus rebuked him for even insinuating that He would go against the commands and the will of God.

Finally, in the natural sense, Jesus would have also been justified in yielding to the third temptation that Satan brought to Him. After all, Jesus was truly the Son of God in the flesh, and that is actually something to brag, boast, and show off about, right? Once again, however, Jesus was so full of God's word that He recognized that the father of sinful pride was trying to get Him to act like a fool. So instead of engaging in a long conversation, He simply stated that we should not test God. This could translate to many situations that Christians get themselves in willfully, without permission from God, but expect God to deliver them or work through them or for them, just because they are so-called "Christians." The temptations of Jesus teach us that, as Christians, we will be faced with many seemingly justifiable reasons or ways to disregard the will of God, but it is always in our best interest to resist all forms of temptation. When we yield to temptation, we sin willfully, and willful sin sets us at odds with our Heavenly Father. Our duty as Christians is to strive to always be in right standing with God.

As true believers, we need to constantly feast and meditate on God's word so that we would be able to withstand any test. Remember that the word of God is the spiritual food that strengthens and nourishes the Holy Spirit that God gave us to be our Helper as we work for the kingdom of God on earth. As children of God, we should "fuel up" on spiritual food more than or just as often as we "fuel up" on natural food, because we need to "walk in the spirit" to avoid fulfilling the lusts of the flesh.

Clear Priorities and Quality Time with God

I believe that every true believer desires to have a closer walk with God, and we all enjoy the presence of God in our lives. However, we do very little to commune with the Spirit of God in us. As with all things, whatever you spend your time practicing or nurturing, that is the thing that will flourish. Let's take a moment to introspect. Do you spend a lot of time on your job, your hair, your makeup, your diet, your car, your personal interests, and hobbies? Well, these are the first things that people will automatically notice about you. As true Christians, God has called us to be representatives of Him on the earth. Therefore, we need to deliberately spend quality time praying, praising, meditating, and studying God's word every day. Consequently, the glory, goodness, and power of God would be the first and lasting impression that people get when they interact with us.

Among some, there seems to be an infectious perpetuation of the idea that we are representing God with our abundance of material possessions or our manicured physical appearances. However, wealthy non-believers can do the same thing, so what sets us apart? We are known as children of God by revealing the glory of God to humankind through our daily lifestyles, our words, our actions, and our endeavors. Does this mean that we should neglect our physical appearances or reject the abundance of material things? Absolutely, not! It simply means that we need to shift our priorities. We need to spend more time developing our "inner-man," which is the part of us that allows us to reflect Christ and realize that the more we have, the more we are expected to be a blessing to others.

Consider what it would be like if we took the time we spent on ourselves and the things we want and devoted it to God and the things of God while taking the time that we would normally spend with God and spent it to ourselves. When we think about it, "the time" we give God certainly is not enough time to do all the things we want, need, and must do for ourselves, right? But who are we? Do we not claim to be yielded vessels unto the Lord God Almighty? So how and when did our needs, interests, and desires become more important than the will of our Creator? As a matter of fact, God only requires that we give Him a tenth of all things, and many of us still struggle with this daily. So, can you imagine the state we would be in if God required ninety percent of all things? Relax, though; God wants us to live abundantly and does not want us to neglect ourselves, our families, or our friends. He is also not irrational, unkind, or unfair. He loves us very much, and ultimately everything we give up or sacrifice for His sake, He gives it back to us. God always outshines us with His giving. As a matter of fact, haven't you noticed that He is always doing more for us than we could ever dream, ask, or imagine? So, let's trust God and watch Him turn things around for us, especially when we learn to put Him first.

We will know that we are becoming less carnally minded when we are able to respond to the wiles of the enemy with appropriate Scripture rather than constantly yielding to temptation. We would move away from constantly making excuses for our flesh or taking for granted the unmerited favor of God. As we mature, we would not be constant victims of Satan's vices because we know that it takes putting on the whole armor of God daily to withstand the attacks of the enemy. It is important that we realize that being human is our reality, but it is no excuse when it comes to the things of God. Jesus was a perfect example of how we should navigate and maneuver in the world. He is our only example and the one after whom we should strive to pattern ourselves. Further, it does not matter how long we have been servants of the Most High; we can never let our guards down. Our adversary is an ancient being who never ceases his attacks, so we have to remain vigilant as long as we have breath in our bodies. Therefore, it is incumbent that we spend quality time seeking God's face so that we can be constantly alert, and when Satan tempts us or attacks us, we can respond in much the same way as Jesus did.

Portraying Our Heavenly Father

On another note, many of us will be held accountable for the way that we present or portray God to others. This means that we either paint a picture of:

a) a ruthlessly fearsome God who desires unreasonable sacrifices and blind obedience, or,

b) a somewhat desperate or weak God who is looking for any and everyone, including counterfeits, to boost his ego and spread a "watered down" version of His word.

However, God is neither ruthlessly fearsome or unreasonable nor desperate and weak. God is good, and He does all things well! He is merciful, faithful, and just! His promises are immutable, and His ways are past finding out! It pays to honor Him with our lives because He is God all by Himself! He is the true ruler and righteous judge of heaven and earth. It is not His will that any man should perish, but that all would come to eternal life. Therefore, He sent His only begotten Son Jesus Christ so that whosoever believes in Him should not perish but have everlasting life. And according to Jesus, He came that we might have life and have it more abundantly (2 Peter 3:9; John 3:16; John 10:10).

As ambassadors for Christ, we must always remember and teach that God is our loving and forgiving Father who wants the best for all humankind. He is the Creator of the heavens and the earth and is therefore rich in all things. As repentant and obedient children who faithfully and unconditionally do the will of our Father, we please Him and, therefore, we experience blessings now and will be privileged to share in His infinitely bountiful supply in the world to come. When we diligently live and share this revelation of God with others, we will become true representatives of Christ and ambassadors for the kingdom of Heaven.

Our Lives Should Bring Glory to God

As children of God, we must also be cautious so as not to suffer the affliction of greed. We should always remember that we have received freely from God, so we should never seek credit for anything we do in Jesus' name. It is God who allows miracles, signs, and wonders to be done in and through us. Therefore, we should never try to steal or share in God's glory. For carnal Christians seeking validity from others, this is sometimes a difficult thing to do. After all, walking with Jesus is like being in constant company with a Superstar. However, walking in the Spirit keeps us grounded and knowledgeable of the fact that God's presence and power have nothing to do with our level of holiness or righteousness, but rather the matchless mercy and grace of God. In moments like these, we should be quick to thank God for the privilege of witnessing, experiencing, and being a part of His great works.

As Christians, we need to remember that sin separates us from our godlike qualities and Godly heritage. However, Jesus died to rectify this disparity, and once we accept Him as Lord and Savior, our duty is to trust God and do His will. In so doing, we will ultimately walk in God-given authority and dominion over the things of this world. This means that humankind does not have to be the victim of any disease or illness, because, through faith, we can obtain full healing and be restored to God's original plan of wholeness for us. Nonetheless, God's promises will not become a reality in our lives until we allow the Holy Spirit to transform our hearts and renew our minds.

As true believers, we should be known as peculiar people. We are called to go the extra mile in everything. We must trust that the power of God within us is greater than any evil in the world. We should also remember that if we always choose to do the minimum or the ordinary, we are not true representatives of Jesus, because the ways of Jesus are always "outside the box." We are called to love more and do more to help those who are in need. We are called to be more patient, more diligent, more enduring, more trustworthy, and more tolerant. However, when it comes to tolerance, it does not mean that we must condone behavior, situations, and practices that are contrary to what the Bible teaches. It only means that we should be more understanding that many people are victims of various forms of oppression, and we need to do whatever we can to lovingly steer them towards the light of Jesus Christ.

Christ-like Tolerance and Homosexuality

When it comes to the treatment of those whose lifestyles and choices are in conflict with nature and God's word, the aim is to be understanding of our human plight, but also unwavering ambassadors for the kingdom of Heaven. For example, in Matthew 19:4-5, Jesus states, "Have you not read that He who made them at the beginning made them male and female, and said, for this reason, a man shall leave his father and mother and be joined to his wife, and the two shall become one flesh?" Hence, I know that the practice of homosexuality is scripturally and scientifically unnatural behavior and is in direct violation of God's plan for His children. Nonetheless, we should not ostracize or condemn individuals who live alternative lifestyles or exhibit homosexual behavior, because these unnatural urges are actually very real to them. Some individuals struggle with their identity and try to keep their homosexual tendencies a secret, which results in promiscuity and other forms of oppressive behavior. On the other hand, many individuals accept this kind of behavior as the new normal, and others are convinced that they were born that way or that God made them that way.

Consequently, without the loving intervention of the Holy Spirit, many of these individuals will remain blissfully unaware that they are the victims of a most deviant and pervasive form of oppression.

However, as true Christians, we can remain unshakably satisfied that God is not fickle and that He does not make mistakes. So, we must hold fast to the belief that the pervasive and seductively oppressive spirit of homosexuality is the direct result of Satan's dark presence and manipulation of the things in this world. As believers, we need to be constantly aware that we live in a world where Satan has the power to interfere with our minds and our emotions. Unclean spirits and generational curses can make lifelong victims of our most vulnerable, receptive, or unsuspecting individuals if they are not rooted and grounded in the belief and power of God and covered by the blood of Jesus Christ.

So, what does a Christian do when faced with a relative, friend, or neighbor who is seduced by and or living the homosexual lifestyle? First of all, as I alluded to earlier, we need to regard homosexual tendencies as a very pervasive and deviant form of oppression that can only be ousted or rendered inactive through the power of God. In addition, we need to remember that the weapons of our warfare are not carnal, for we do not wrestle against flesh and blood. So, harsh words, derogatory terms, criticism, and endless debates are moot points. Also, we should treat these individuals with respect, show them love, and spend time in their company. All the while, we should be mindful that when we do these things, it is not to condone or encourage the homosexual lifestyle or tendencies, but to have similar results as those that Jesus had when He came into contact with sinners. Jesus' comportment with sinners was much different from His manner towards corrupt spiritual leaders and those who should know better. Therefore, sinners were transformed whenever they had an encounter with Him.

Consequently, the believer's primary response is to fast and pray fervently that individuals with these tendencies have a genuine encounter with Christ. The Bible teaches us that no matter how hedonistic or depraved an individual may seem, one encounter with Jesus can literally transform that individual forever. In

Luke 19:1-10, we see how Zacchaeus, a well-known extortioner, was compelled to change his ways after only one meal with Jesus. In John 4 we read about Jesus' encounter with the Samaritan woman at the well and in John 8:1-11 we read the account of Jesus and the woman caught in the act of adultery. Jesus' compassionate response to these women and their plight caused both women to transition into a newness of life. In Acts 9, we read of how Saul, a prominent persecutor of the early Christians, had a change of heart after his encounter with Christ on the road to Damascus. These are just a few biblical accounts of individuals who made a complete turnaround due to their encounter with Christ. This is proof that there is no limit to the kind of deliverance Christ can provide for those who are lost or victims of varying forms of oppression. There is no sinner who interacted with Jesus who remained clueless or whose life was not transformed eventually.

Some may argue that Jesus never spoke out against homosexuality, so there must not be anything wrong with it. But I am here to point out this fact. The scribes and the Pharisees followed Moses' Law to the letter, which meant that the practice of homosexuality and other named abominations against God were not up for debate in Jesus' day. However, Jesus did weigh in on subjects like divorce and adultery to eliminate the ambiguity regarding these matters. Nonetheless, be not deceived. God is not mocked. He is the same yesterday, today, and forever. Therefore, the same things that were an abomination to Him in the Old Testament are still an abomination to Him today. Hence, the only way to be in right standing with God is to repent, accept Jesus Christ as Lord and Savior, be cleansed from all unrighteousness, and henceforth live in a manner that is pleasing in the eyes of God, with the help of the Holy Spirit. Unfortunately, anyone who resists this way or tries to create a new path is deceived and willfully chooses to spend eternity separated from God.

On the other hand, a Christian who struggles with homosexual desires and tendencies should accept that these urges are outside the will of God. As believers, we know that homosexuality falls in the category of every other lust of the flesh that should be avoided. According to 1 Corinthians 6: 9-20, all sexual immorality is sin and when we yield to these desires, we are among the unrighteous who will not inherit the kingdom of God. Further, we are admonished to flee fornication and view our bodies as temples of the Holy Spirit. We know that outside of marriage, sexual acts between heterosexuals and homosexuals are considered fornication and/or adultery. We also know that God only ordains marriage between a man and a woman. So, even if the believer claims to be married to someone of the same gender, that marriage is not recognized by God. Therefore, the sexual acts within that marriage are still a sin. So, apart from divine and total deliverance from these desires, the believer who struggles with these tendencies should remain celibate and continue resisting with prayers. According to James 4:7, when we are assailed by any form of temptation, we should submit ourselves to the Lord, resist the devil and he will flee from us. I have heard it said that homosexual relationships can be very loving, rewarding and may even be sexually gratifying, but we should remember that all temptations appeal to the flesh in one way or the other. Consequently, Galatians 6: 7-8 warns believers not to be deceived because God is not mocked. It is indicated that when we sow in the flesh, we reap corruption but when we sow in the Spirit, we reap everlasting life. Therefore, when it comes to sinful desires, and the lusts of our old sinful nature, let us strive to be transformed daily by the renewing of our minds and the rebirth made possible by the cleansing power of the blood of Jesus our Savior.

Christ-like Perspective on Infirmities and Disabilities

As a Christian, I also do not believe that we are meant to accept the many disabilities and infirmities that we experience or witness in our loved ones and other individuals as "the norm" for God's kingdom. If infirmities and disabilities are acceptable as a way of life for God's children, then why was Jesus' ministry one of healing and deliverance? If you believe that an imperfect world where people suffer and are victims of oppression is what God intended for His children, then you will never be delivered from the mindset that is hindering you from the life of abundance that God wants you to have in and through Christ Jesus. If it was God's will for His children to suffer without relief or a way of escape, Christ would never have come to Earth with the anointing and mandate outlined in Isaiah 61, and such a mandate would not have been passed on the followers of Jesus Christ (Mark 16:17). Therefore, we must believe unwaveringly that Christ died to correct the anomalies in our lives and that once we accept Him as our Lord and Savior, we are entitled to deliverance from oppression in every area of our lives. We need to have unwavering faith that the blood of Jesus can deliver all of God's children from all forms of bondage and oppression.

So, even if many of us do not receive our healing or deliverance in this world, it would certainly be a part of our reward in the world to come. On the other hand, I do believe that there are many individuals who are meant to be delivered from their infirmities and disabilities in this life. Therefore, in many cases, the laying on of hands, for others the prayer of faith, and for some, the effectual fervent prayer of the righteous servants of God, avails much to bring about these types of deliverances (James 5:15 & 16). In the meantime, we need to remember that our Savior always had compassion for those who are less fortunate as well as those individuals with various handicaps or disabilities. Therefore, as Christians, we should always endeavor to do whatever we can to help these individuals feel valued and make their lives more meaningful, comfortable, and enjoyable.

Further, for those who are living with disabilities, I do not claim to understand the difficulty, but I do know that it is not healthy to think subjectively. In John 9, when Jesus was asked whose sin caused the man to be born blind, Jesus answered that it was not anyone's fault, but rather that the works of God could be revealed in him. I also encourage you to be comforted by the testimony of the Apostle Paul in 2 Corinthians 12:7-10. Verse 9 reads, "And He said to me, 'My grace is sufficient for you, for My strength is made perfect in weakness.' Therefore most gladly I will rather boast in my infirmities, that the power of Christ may rest upon me." I believe that it is the duty of a Christian, regardless of status or ability, to view our situations as an opportunity to bring glory to God. Therefore, if you are not already doing so, pray for strength and for the works of Christ and the glory of God to be revealed through you. After all, 1 Thessalonians 5:18 reminds us that "in everything give thanks; for this is the will of God in Christ Jesus concerning you."

Jesus is Present for The Believer

Many Christians forget to look to Jesus for everything. They go about their daily lives as if the God of the Bible has changed and that He is somehow limited or powerless to deal with the circumstances and situations that they are faced with. They forget that Jesus walked this earth in human form and has unquestionable knowledge of what human beings are faced with on earth. We disregard the fact that as the Son of God who gave His life for us, He now sits at the right hand of the Father interceding on our behalf. There are also Christians who are aware of God's power, but they think that His promises and ability to deliver are either deferred until they get to Heaven or reserved for a "selected few."

On the other hand, there are those of us who constantly trust the wisdom, ability, and strength of individuals and readily lean on our own understanding rather than exercising faith in God. Let us not be like the Israelites in the Old Testament. Despite the fact that God repeatedly delivered them in ways that were beyond human comprehension, they quickly forgot and went about their lives as if their health, wealth, and safety were a result of their own wisdom and might. Their hard-headed and stiff-necked ways led to a lot of unnecessary deaths, heartaches, and hardships. Let us be wise and learn from the mistakes of the Israelites and unwaveringly look to Jesus and trust God for all things.

Jesus is Our Example and The Answer

As true believers, we need to be mindful that in all of Jesus' teachings and behavior, He never disregarded any of the commandments of God. Instead, He disputed the prevailing and preferred traditions of the religious leaders, who were motivated by their own self-righteous standards. The commandments were given as a heavenly standard of living and were intended to keep humankind mindful of and dependent upon their Heavenly Father. The penalty for breaking any commandment was immediate or gradual death. Sin is an abomination to God and, therefore, sin and everything associated with it must be destroyed or permanently removed from the presence of the Lord. The story of Noah and The Flood (Genesis 7-9) and the story of Sodom and Gomorrah (Genesis 19) serve as testaments to this fact. However, every human being since Adam was born in sin and therefore is destined to die. So how could human beings, who are slaves to sin, please a Holy God? The only way for any human being to please God is to obey Him even unto death and unfailingly keep His commandments, which proves impossible. Fortunately for us, Jesus Christ is the only human who was ever able to do this, and He is the only acceptable sacrifice that nullifies the "debt of death" for all humankind. As Christ's ambassadors, we must believe and accept this gift through faith and share this revelation with those who are lost.

As born-again believers and children of the Living God, we should always trust God and remember His source of reconciliation back to Him. God gave us His Son Jesus Christ, and when we accept Jesus into our hearts, God only sees Jesus when He looks at us. Jesus is who and what we have! Christ in us makes us more than conquerors in this world. We can do nothing good in and of ourselves. Therefore, it is crucial for every believer to realize the power and the privilege that we have in and because of Jesus Christ. Jesus is our all. Without Him, all our doing, living, and believing is in vain.

Jesus is our teacher, our healer, our righteousness, our purpose, our joy, our hope, our light, our redeemer, our salvation, and our only way of escape from eternal damnation. As long as we keep Him in our focus, we can walk on water and smile at the storm. With Jesus, anything is possible. However, if we allow ourselves to be distracted or deceived and take our eyes of Jesus, the burdens of this life will overwhelm us and cause us to sink into a sea of fear, doubt, and despair. As born-again believers, even when our natural perceptions may indicate otherwise, we must constantly meditate on the fact that "we can do all things through Christ who strengthens us" (Philippians 4:13). It is in Jesus! With Jesus as the nucleus of our existence, we can experience days of heaven on this earth. Our health, businesses, marriages, offspring, relationships, and endeavors are all blessed in, through, and because of Jesus.

Jesus, the Antidote

God looked upon this earth ages ago and saw His creation going around in circles and being victims at Satan's disposal in every area of their lives. He saw the lack of real and lasting vision, hope, joy, and satisfaction. Everything was out of order, and humans were slaves to sin and oppression in thought and deed, a state that Satan had perpetuated in the world so that we would always be under his subjection. However, God always knew the purpose and potential of His creation and knew that once we were provided with a way of escape, we would indeed awaken from our stupor and shake off the oppression of the enemy. Therefore, He rescued us from the hands and the plans of the enemy. "He sent His only begotten Son, so that whoever believes in Him would not perish but have everlasting life" (John 3:16). Jesus was and is the ultimate sacrifice. He gave His life as a ransom to redeem us.

As human beings, we are all created in the image of God. However, only Christ's blood can resurrect the Godlike qualities that lie dormant within us. Without Christ, we can only be counterfeits, even in our goodness. As a result of Adam's disobedience, we have been saddled with a sinful nature. This means that despite our Godlike potential, we only reflect devilish qualities and are subject to satanic oppression unless we recognize, accept, and embrace the light that is in Jesus Christ.

Triumphing Daily

Resting in Jesus and trusting in His ability to provide for us, protect and deliver us, result in victories in every area of a true believer's life. I have personally experienced loss, disappointments, situations, and circumstances that could and perhaps would devastate and unravel the sanity of most human beings. In instances where counseling and therapy would have been required to help some individuals get over their pain, the Holy Spirit acted as a buffer which shielded me in the face of adversity. Moreover, because I have learned to trust in Jesus and look to Him for deliverance, these experiences have only served to strengthen and fortify me spiritually. It is because of praying, praising, and trusting in God that the enemy's attacks that were meant to destroy me and my faith in God were of little or no consequence. Hence, I am confident that "with Christ in the vessel, we can truly smile at the storm." So, if or when I am struck with any form of adversity, I know and can say with certainty, "this too shall pass."

Once we accept Jesus Christ as our Lord and Savior, we must adopt a new mindset by trading in our sorrows, sicknesses, pain, and shame for the joy, peace, and victory that is in Christ Jesus. It also means that, like Paul, we would not become burdened or oppressed because of the hardships and disappointments we may experience in this world. Instead, we would exercise hope and faith in the belief that "this too shall pass" and be mindful of a much better life on earth as well as all the rewards in Heaven. As born-again believers, our manual, the Bible, tells us that the faithful are going to reign with Christ. The Bible is inspired by God. God cannot lie, and He would not allow a lie to be perpetuated in His name. Therefore, if we endure to the end, we can rest assured that we will reap great rewards on earth as well as in the world to come.

Jesus is The Way, The Truth and The Light

We must remember that Jesus Christ is the only way back to God and our only hope of eternal life. Hence, it is prudent to accept Him by faith into our hearts as our Lord and Savior if we ever expect to enter the kingdom of Heaven. It is also critical for every believer who has accepted the gift of salvation through Jesus Christ to activate the power of the Holy Spirit in their lives so that they can live victoriously and fulfill their purpose on earth. Remember that Jesus is "The Way," "The Truth," and "The Light," and without Him, we remain under oppression and are lost in captivity and sin. Without Jesus Christ our Savior, we are powerless against Satan, and humankind can only look forward to death and eternal damnation. But, as Jesus said, He came that we might have life and have it more abundantly (John 10:10). This abundant life refers to our joy, peace of mind, and prosperity in this life, as well as the hope of eternal life in the kingdom of Heaven. We must also trust in and rest in the words of our Lord and Savior when He says, "Come to Me, all you who labor and are heavy laden, and I will give you rest. Take My yoke upon you and learn from Me, for I am gentle and lowly in heart, and you will find rest for your souls. For My yoke is easy and My burden is light" (Matthew 11:28-30). As born-again believers, we can only experience true liberty and complete victory when we bask in the amazing gift of Jesus Christ, who enables us to tap into the power of God, allows us to have dominion over the things in this world, guarantees us a place in Heaven, reinstates us to a position of authority, and affords us the privilege of being called children of the Most High God!

Jesus is The Rock of Our Salvation

As we go about our lives every day trying to exemplify the character of Christ and doing the will of God, we must be ever mindful that we can never endure to the end or finish this race without Divine help. As human beings, we will sometimes be assailed by doubt. Occasionally, we will even question our faith. Despair will threaten to overtake us in some situations. Despite our best intentions, we will often get weary in well-doing. We will frequently be tempted to relapse into our old selfish and self-serving ways. We will continue to realize that we are not perfect, no matter how hard we try. We will always have to apply deliberate effort into disciplining our minds, our emotions, and our bodies until the day we die.

Furthermore, we must never forget that we are subject to all these things and more because Satan is very determined to make it extremely difficult and almost impossible for any Christian to fight the good fight of faith, finish this race, or endure to the end. Fortunately, Jesus is aware of our plight, and He knows all about our struggles. Yet, He does not want us to use our human nature as an excuse to "cop-out," act like victims, and continue living in sin.

Instead, we need to cling to Jesus and strictly adhere to the words He spoke in Matthew 26:41: "Watch and pray, lest you enter into temptation. The spirit is willing, but the flesh is weak." As believers, we have the supreme antidote that makes it possible to endure all things and be overcomers in every situation. Therefore, let us continue to focus on Jesus, meditate on His words, and lift Him up. He is the One who intercedes on our behalf. He is the One who recharges us and provides us with the ammunition we need to be victorious in the battlefields of our hearts, bodies, and minds. So, keep the faith! Stay true to God and trust that Jesus is indeed the Rock of our salvation!

For more Scriptural study related to this chapter, go to page 161.

CHAPTER 10

C-R-A-Z-Y—The Acronym

Own Your CRAZY

I am C-R-A-Z-Y: **C**hrist of Calvary, **R**ansomed and Redeemed, **A**nointed and Appointed, **Z**ealous, and **Y**ielded! Which combination of "C-R-A-Z-Y" best defines your relationship with God and/or your status as a believer in Christ?

The 'C' in CRAZY:

Christ—The One sent by God to die for my sins.

Calvary—The place where Christ was crucified for my sins

Christian—A follower of Jesus Christ

Connected—My relationship with God because of The Christ of Calvary.

Committed—My stance as it relates to the things of God

Consecrated—Set aside to do the will of the LORD

Conqueror—Is what I am in and because of Jesus Christ

Called—Obedient to the voice of The Good Shepherd

Chosen—A disciple of Jesus Christ

Captivated—Stuck on Jesus

Confident—That I can do all things through Christ who strengthens me.

Considered—Not discounted and sidelined because of circumstance.

Complete—Is how I feel when I am in the presence of The Lord.

Commissioned—An agent of the Living God, granted the power to carry out specific acts and duties on this earth in the name of my Lord and Savior Jesus Christ

The 'R' in CRAZY:

Ransomed—Freed from captivity and punishment and because of Jesus' blood.

Redeemed—Brought with a price and rescued from sin because of Jesus' blood.

Restored—Brought back to an earlier or original state of innocence.

Reinstated—To place again in a former position or condition.

Re-established—To bring into being and to put beyond doubt again.

Revolutionized—Greatly and completely changed because of knowing God.

Revived—Brought back to a freshness of life, activity, and consciousness.

Reverent—Very respectful of the commands and statutes of The Living God.

Renewed—Been made like new, fresh and strong again.

Reunited—Brought back together with my heavenly Father.

Refreshed—Made fresh.

Rich—Wealthy in all good things.

Rehearsed—Practiced in private for in preparation for public performance.

Righteous—Being or doing what is right.

Radical—Departing sharply from the usual or ordinary.

The 'A' in CRAZY:

Anointed—Covered by the blood of Jesus and full of the Spirit of God.

Appointed—Chosen by God to work in the vineyards of the world.

Affirmed—Confidently declaring my ransomed state of existence in, through, and because of Jesus!

Awed—Filled with mixed feelings of fear, respect, and wonder for God!

Authorized—Given authority and empowered by The Living God.

Approved—Accepted by God as fitting and satisfactory for His service.

Amazed—Greatly surprised at God's abounding love, mercy, favor, grace, faithfulness, patience, and forgiveness toward humanity.

Armed—Equipped with the word of God as a way of defense.

Available—Always obtainable and usable by God.

Aware—Showing and having an understanding and knowledge of the goodness of God.

Alert—In a constant state of readiness to defend my freedom in Jesus Christ.

The 'Z' in CRAZY:

Zestful—Excited and enjoying the presence of God in my life.

Zealous—Eager and filled with a strong desire to please God and do His will upon the earth.

Zippy—Always lively, full of energy, and ready to do all things well.

The 'Y' in CRAZY:

Youthful—Young at heart, having the freshness of youth and childlike in my dependency and trust in God.

Yearning—Filled with an eager desire to be close to God, have more of God, and be more like Christ.

Yielded—A servant of The Living God, sold out to His will and purpose!

Scripture References

Categorized for Deeper Study and Meditation

Light & Life (Chapter 2)

And I will give you the keys of the kingdom of heaven, and whatever you bind on earth will be bound in heaven, and whatever you loose on earth will be loosed in heaven (Matthew 16:19).

Assuredly, I say to you, whatever you bind on earth will be bound in heaven, whatever you loose on earth will be loosed in heaven. Again I say to you that if two of you agree on earth concerning anything that they ask, it will be done for them by My Father in heaven (Matthew 18:18-19).

For I will give you a mouth and wisdom which all your adversaries will not be able to contradict or resist…And you will be hated by all for My name's sake. But not a hair of your head shall be lost (Luke 21:15 & 17-18).

Most assuredly, I say to you, he who believes in Me, the works that I do he will do also; and greater works than these he will do, because I go to My Father. And whatever you ask in My name, that I will do, that the Father may be glorified in the Son. If you ask anything in My name, I will do it (John 14:12-14).

You are My friends if you do whatever I command you. You did not choose Me, but I chose you and appointed you that you should go and bear fruit, and that your fruit should remain, that whatever you ask the Father in My name He may give you (John 15:14 & 16).

I do not pray for these alone, but for those who will believe in Me through their word; that they all may be one, as You, Father, are in Me, and I in You; that they may be one in Us, that the world may believe that You sent Me (John 17:20-21).

But you shall receive power when the Holy Spirit has come upon you; and you shall be witnesses to Me in Jerusalem, and in all Judea and Samaria, and to the end of the earth (Acts 1:8).

Now He who establishes us with you in Christ and has anointed you in Christ and has anointed us is God, who also has sealed us and given us the Spirit in our hearts (2 Corinthians 1:21-22).

Behold, O My people, I will open your graves and cause you to come up from your graves, and bring you into the land of Israel. Then you shall know that I am the Lord, when I have opened your graves, O My people, and brought you up from your graves (Ezekiel 37:12-13).

Then you shall know that I am in the midst of Israel; I am the Lord your God and there is no other. My people shall never be put to shame (Joel 2:27).

I can do all things through Christ who strengthens me (Philippians 4:13).

The mystery which has been hidden from ages and from generations, but now has been revealed to His saints. To them God willed to make known what are the riches of the glory of this mystery among the Gentiles:which is Christ in you, the hope of glory (Colossians 1:26-27).

According to Titus 2:14, Our Savior Jesus Christ "who gave Himself for us, that He might redeem us from every lawless deed and purify for Himself His own special people, zealous for good works".

The kindness and love of God appeared unto us "not by works

of righteousness which we have done, but according to His mercy He saved us through the washing of regeneration and renewing of the Holy Spirit" (Titus 3:5).

God says "Fear not, for I have redeemed you; I have called you by your name; you are Mine" (Isaiah 43:1).

But the natural man does not receive the things of the Spirit of God, for they are foolishness to him; nor can he know them, because they are spiritually discerned (1 Corinthians 2:14).

What shall we say to these things? If God is for us, who can be against us (Romans 8:31).

The God of our fathers raised up Jesus whom you murdered by hanging on a tree. Him God has exalted to His right hand to be Prince and Savior, to give repentance to Israel and forgiveness of sins. And we are His witnesses to these things, and so also is the Holy Spirit whom God has given to those who obey Him (Acts 5:30-32).

But he who looks into the perfect law of liberty and continues in it, and is not a forgetful hearer but a doer of the work, this one will be blessed in what he does (James 1:25).

But I am the Lord your God, who divided the sea whose waves roared: The Lord of hosts is His name. And I have put My words in your mouth; I have covered you with the shadow of My hand (Isaiah 51:15-16).

The Lord God is my strength; He will make my feet like deer's feet, and He will make me walk on high hills (Habakkuk 3:19).

A man's gift makes room for him, and brings him before great men (Proverbs 18:16).

You are of God, little children, and have overcome them, because He who is in you is greater than he who is in the world (1 John 4:4).

You are My servant, I have chosen you and have not cast you away; Fear not, for I am with you; be not dismayed, for I am your God. I will strengthen you, yes, I will help you. I will uphold you with My righteous right hand (Isaiah 41:9-10).

I will greatly rejoice in the Lord, My soul shall be joyful in my God; for He has clothed me with the garments of salvation. He has covered me with the robe of righteousness (Isaiah 61:10).

Let the words of my mouth and the meditation of my heart be acceptable in Your sight, O Lord, my strength and my redeemer (Psalm 19:14).

My Spirit who is upon you, and My words which I have put in your mouth, shall not depart from your mouth, nor the mouth of your descendants, nor from the mouth of your descendants' descendants, says the Lord, from this time and forevermore (Isaiah 59:21).

HEAVENLY WISDOM, PART 1 (CHAPTER 3)

Take heed to yourselves. If your brother sins against you, rebuke him; and if he repents, forgive him. And if he sins against you seven times in a day, and seven times in a day returns to you, saying, 'I repent', you shall forgive him (Luke 17:3-4).

So likewise you, when you have done all those things which you are commanded, say, 'We are unprofitable servants. We have done what was our duty to do (Luke 17:10).

So I say to you, ask and it will be given to you; seek, and you will find; knock, and it will be opened to you (Luke 11:9).

If you then, being evil, know how to give good gifts to your children, how much more will your heavenly Father give the Holy Spirit to those who ask Him (Luke 11:13)!

But love your enemies, do good and lend, hoping for nothing in return; and your reward will be great, and you will be sons of the Most High. For He is kind to the unthankful and evil. Therefore be merciful, just as your Father also is merciful (Luke 6:35-36).

Therefore whoever hears these sayings of Mine, and does them, I will liken him to a wise man who built his house on the rock:and the rain descended, the floods came, and the winds blew and beat on that house; and it did not fall, for it was founded on the rock (Matthew 7:24).

Give and it will be given to you:good measure, pressed down, shaken together, running over will be put into your bosom. For with the same measure that you use it, it will be measured back to you (Luke 6:38).

But is you had known what this means, I desire mercy and not sacrifice, you would not have condemned the guiltless (Matthew 12:7).

Judge not, and you shall not be judged. Condemn not, and you shall not be condemned. Forgive and you will be forgiven (Luke 6:37).

Then the King will say to those on His right hand, 'Come you blessed of My Father, inherit the kingdom prepared for you from the foundation of the world:for I was hungry and you gave me food; I was thirsty and you gave Me drink; I was a stranger and you took Me in; I was naked and you clothed Me; I was sick and you visited Me; I was in prison and you came to Me (Matthew 25:34-36).

Let the little children come to Me, and do not forbid them; for of such is the kingdom of God. Assuredly, I say to you, whoever does not receive the kingdom of God as a little child will by no means enter it (Mark 10:14-15).

Those who are well have no need of a physician, but those who are sick. I did not come to call the righteous, but sinners to repentance (Mark 2:17).

And whenever you stand praying, if you have anything against anyone, forgive him, that your Father in heaven may also forgive you your trespasses. But if you do not forgive, neither will your Father in heaven forgive your trespasses (Mark 11:25-26).

He who is of God hears God's words; therefore you do not hear, because you are not of God (John 8:47).

Simon, son of Jonah, do you love Me more than these? Feed My lambs. Simon, son of Jonah, do you love Me? Tend My sheep. Simon, son of Jonah, do you love Me? Do you love Me? Feed My sheep (John 21:15-17).

I will arise and go to my father, and will say to him, Father, I have sinned against heaven and before you, and I am no longer worthy to be called your son. Make me like one of your hired servants. And he arose and came to his father. But when he was still a great way off, his father saw him and had compassion, and ran and fell on his neck and kissed him (Luke 15:18-20).

Is this not the fast that I have chosen:to loose the bonds of wickedness, to undo the heavy burdens, to let the oppressed go free, and that you break every yoke? Is it not to share your bread with the hungry, and that you bring to your house the poor who are cast out; when you see the naked, that you cover him, and not hide yourself from your own flesh (Isaiah 58:6-7).

Then your light shall break forth like the morning, your healing shall spring forth speedily, and your righteousness shall go before you; The glory of the Lord shall be your rear guard. Then you shall call, and the Lord will answer; you shall cry, and He will say, 'Here I am' (Isaiah 58:8-9).

What does it profit, my brethren, if someone says he has faith but does not have works? Can faith save him? If a brother or sister is naked and destitute of daily food, and one of you says to them, "Depart in peace, be warmed and filled, but you do not give them the things which are needed for the body, what does it profit? Thus also faith by itself, if it does not have works, is dead (James 2:14-17).

For this is the will of God, that by doing good you may put to silence the ignorance of foolish men:as free, yet not abusing liberty as a cloak or vice, but as bondservants of God. Honor al people. Love the brotherhood. Fear God. Honor the king (1 Peter 2:15-17).

For if you thoroughly amend your ways and your doings, if you thoroughly execute judgment between a man and his neighbor, if you do not oppress the stranger, the fatherless, and the widow, and do not shed innocent blood in this place, or walk after other gods to your hurt, then I will cause you to dwell in this place, in the land that I gave to your fathers forever and ever (Jeremiah 7:5-7).

God stands in the congregation of the mighty; He judges among the gods. How long will you judge unjustly, and show partiality to the wicked? Defend the poor and the fatherless; do justice to the afflicted and needy. Deliver the poor and needy; free them from the hand of the wicked (Psalm 82:1-4).

They do not know, nor do they understand; they walk about in darkness; all the foundations of the earth are unstable (Psalm 82:5).

I said, you are gods, and all of you are children of the Most High, but you shall die like men, and fall like one of the princes (Psalm 82:6-7).

Love never fails. But whether there are prophecies, they will fail; whether there are tongues they will cease; whether there is knowledge, it will vanish away (1 Corinthians 13:8).

Scripture References

For I am persuaded that neither death nor life, nor angels nor principalities nor powers, nor things present nor things to come, nor height nor depth, nor any other created thing, shall be able to separate us from the love of God which is in Christ Jesus our Lord (Romans 8:38-39).

Let each of you look out not only for his own interests, but also for the interests of others (Philippians 2:4).

Let this mind be in you which was also in Christ Jesus, who, being in the form of God, did not consider it robbery to be equal with God, but made Himself of no reputation, taking the form of a bondservant, and coming in the likeness of men. And being found in appearance as a man, He humbled Himself and became obedient to the point of death, even the death of the cross (Philippians 2:5-8).

Pure and undefiled religion before God and the Father is this:to visit orphans and widows in their trouble, and keep oneself unspotted from the world (James 1:27).

And seek the peace of the city where I have caused you to be carried away captive, and pray to the Lord for it; for in its peace you will have peace (Jeremiah 29:7).

For I know the thoughts that I think toward you, says the Lord, thoughts of peace and not of evil, to give you a future and hope. Then you will call upon Me and go and pray to Me, and I will listen to you. And you will seek Me and find Me, when you search for Me with all your heart (Jeremiah 29:11-13).

For all the law is fulfilled in one word, even this:You shall love your neighbor as yourself (Galatians 5:14).

Brethren, if a man is overtaken in any trespass, you who are spiritual restore such a one in a spirit of gentleness, considering yourself lest you also be tempted (Galatians 6:1).

The Lord is merciful and gracious, slow to anger, and abounding in mercy. For as the heavens are high above the earth, so great is His mercy toward those who fear Him (Psalm 103:8 & 11).

For we ourselves were also once foolish, disobedient, deceived, serving various lusts and pleasures, living in malice and envy, hateful and hating one another. But when the kindness and love of God our Savior toward man appeared, not by works of righteousness which we have done, but according to His mercy He saved us, through the washing of regeneration and renewing of the Holy Spirit (Titus 3:3-5).

That having been justified by His grace we should become heirs according to the hope of eternal life (Titus 3:7).

What is man that you are mindful of him, or the son of man that You take care of him? You have made him a little lower than the angels; you have crowned him with glory and honor, and set him over the works of Your hands. You have put all things in subjection under his feet (Hebrews 2:6-8).

Seek God and not evil, that you may live; so the Lord God of hosts will be with you, as you have spoken (Amos 5:14).

I hate, I despise your feast days, and do not savor your sacred assemblies, though you offer Me burnt offerings and your grain offerings, I do not accept them. Nor will I regard your fattened peace offerings. Take away from Me the noise of your songs, for I will not hear the melody of your stringed instruments. But let justice run down like water and righteousness like a stream (Amos 5:21-24).

For I desire mercy and not sacrifice and the knowledge of God more than burnt offerings (Hosea 6:6).

I drew them with gentle cords, with bands of love, and I was to them as those who take the yoke from their neck. I stooped and fed them (Hosea 11:4).

Scripture References

My heart churns within Me; My sympathy is stirred. I will not execute the fierceness of My anger. For I am God and not man the Holy one in your midst; and I will not come with terror (Hosea 11:8-9).

I will heal their backsliding, I will love them freely, for My anger has turned away from him (Hosea 14:4).

Then I will give them one heart, and I will put a new spirit within them, and take the stony heart out of their flesh, and give them a heart of flesh, that they may walk in My statutes and keep My judgments and do them; and they shall be My people, and I will be their God (Ezekiel 11:19-20).

Jude reminds us that "there would be mockers in the last time who would walk according too their own ungodly lusts. These are sensual persons, who cause divisions, not having the Spirit (Jude 1:18-19).

Lord what is man, that you take knowledge of him? Or the son of man, that You are mindful of him? Man is like a breath; his days are like a passing shadow (Psalm 144:3-4).

But the salvation of the righteous is from the Lord; He is their strength in the time of trouble. And the Lord shall help them and deliver them; He shall deliver them from the wicked, and save them, because they trust Him (Psalm 37:39-40).

When I say to the wicked, 'You shall surely die,' and you give him no warning, nor speak to warn the wicked from his wicked way, to save his life, that same wicked man shall die in his iniquity; but his blood I will require at your hand (Ezekiel 3:18).

Now no chastening seems to be joyful for the present, but painful; nevertheless, afterward it yields the peaceable fruit of righteousness to those who have been trained by it (Hebrews 12:11).

My son, do not despise the chastening of the Lord, Nor be discouraged when you are rebuked by Him; for whom the Lord loves He chastens, and scourges every son whom He receives (Hebrews 12:5-6).

But the natural man does not receive the things of the Spirit of God, for they are foolishness to him; nor can he know them, because they are spiritually discerned (1 Corinthians 2:14).

HEAVENLY WISDOM, PART 2 (CHAPTER 3)

Why, when I came, was there no man? Why, when I called, was there none to answer? Is My hand shortened at all that it cannot redeem? Or have I no power to deliver? Indeed with My rebuke I dry up the sea, I make the rivers a wilderness; their fish stink because there is no water, and die of thirst (Isaiah 50:2).

Behold, the Lord's hand is not shortened, that it cannot save; nor His ear heavy, that it cannot hear. But your iniquities have separated you from your God (Isaiah 59:1).

O, taste and see that the Lord is good; blessed is the man who trusts in Him! Oh fear the Lord you His saints! There is no want to those who fear Him. The young lions lack and suffer hunger; But those who seek the Lord shall not lack any good thing (Psalm 34:8-10).

Trust in the Lord, and do good; dwell in the land, and feed on His faithfulness. Delight yourself also in the Lord, and He shall give you the desires of your heart (Psalm 37:3-4).

Trust in the Lord, and do good; dwell in the land, and feed on His faithfulness. Delight yourself also in the Lord, and He shall give you the desires of your heart (Psalm 37:3-4).

The steps of a good man are ordered by the Lord, and He delights in his way. Though he fall, he shall not be utterly cast

Scripture References

down; for the Lord upholds him with His hand (Psalm 37:23-24).

Son of man, when a land sins against Me by persistent unfaithfulness, I will stretch out My hand against it; I will cut off its supply of bread, send famine on it, and cut off man and beast from it (Ezekiel 14:13).

Fear God and keep His commandments, for this is man's all. For God will bring every work into judgment. Including every secret thing, whether good or evil (Ecclesiastes 12:13-14).

These things indeed have an appearance of wisdom in self-imposed religion, false humility, and neglect of the body, but are of no value against the indulgence of the flesh (Colossians 2:23).

For there is one God and one Mediator between God and men, the Man Christ Jesus, who gave Himself a ransom for all, to be testified in due time (1 Timothy 2:5-6).

My brethren, count it all joy when you fall into various trials, knowing that the testing of your faith produces patience. But let patience have its perfect work, that you may be perfect and complete, lacking nothing (James 1:3-4).

If any of you lacks wisdom let him ask God, who gives to all liberally and without reproach, and it will be given to him. But let him ask in faith, with no doubting, for he who doubts is like a wave of the sea driven and tossed by the wind (James 1:5-6).

Blessed is the man who trusts in the Lord, and those whose hope is the Lord. For he shall be like a tree planted by the waters, which spreads out its roots by the river, and it will not fear when heat comes; But its leaf is green, and will not be anxious in the year of drought, nor will cease from yielding fruit (Jeremiah 17:7-8).

The fool says in his heart, "There is no God". They are corrupt, and have done abominable iniquity; there is none who does good (Psalm 53:1).

After first hand experience of the power of God, Nebuchadnezzar blessed the Lord saying, His dominion is an everlasting dominion, and His Kingdom is from generation to generation. All the inhabitants of the earth are reputed as nothing; He does according to His will in the army of heaven and among the inhabitants of the earth. No one can restrain His hand or say to Him, What have You done? (Daniel 4:34-35).

But I discipline my body and bring it into subjection, lest when I have preached to others, I myself should become disqualified (1 Corinthians 9:27).

Let no one deceive himself. If anyone among you seems to be wise in this age, let him become a fool that he may become wise. For the wisdom of this world is foolishness with God. For it is written, "He catches the wise in their own craftiness" and again, "The lord knows the thoughts of the wise, that they are futile (1 Corinthians 3:18-20).

We should always be mindful of Paul's sound advice that "your faith should not be in the wisdom of men but in the power of God" (1 Corinthians 2:5).

Walk in wisdom toward those who are outside, redeeming the time. Let you speech always be with grace, seasoned with salt that you may know how you ought to answer each (Colossians 4:5-6).

Put on the who armor of God, that you may be able to stand against the wiles of the devil. For we do not wrestle against flesh and blood, but against principalities, against powers, against the rulers of the darkness of this age, against spiritual hosts of wickedness in high places (Ephesians 6:11-12).

Romans 10:13 states, "For whoever calls on the name of the Lord shall be saved".

Romans 10:11 states, "Whoever believes on Him will not be put to shame."

Scripture References

The good news of the gospel requires us to preach repentance toward God and faith toward our Lord Jesus Christ (Acts 20:21).

For grace you have been saved through faith, and that not of yourselves; it is the gift of God, not of works, lest anyone should boast (Ephesians 2:8-9).

The fear of the Lord is the beginning of wisdom; a good understanding have all those who do His commandments (Psalms 111:10).

Ezekiel 20:9 states, "But I acted for My name's sake, that it should not be profaned before the Gentiles among whom they were, in whose sight I had made myself known to them, to bring them out of the land of Egypt".

So shall they fear the name of The Lord from the west, and His glory from the rising of the sun; when the enemy comes in like a flood, The spirit of the Lord will lift up a standard against him (Isaiah 59:19).

"God is our refuge and strength, a very present help in trouble" (Psalm 46:1).

3 John 1:11 admonishes us to "not imitate what is evil, but what is good. He who does good is of God, but he who does evil has not seen God".

Who is wise? Let him understand these things. Who is prudent? Let him know them. For the ways of the Lord are right; the righteous walk in them, but transgressors stumble in them (Hosea 14:9).

But if a man is just and does what is lawful and right, nor defiled his neighbors wife, nor approached a woman during her impurity; If he has not oppressed anyone, but has restored to the debtor his pledge; has robbed no one by violence, but has given his bread to the hungry and has covered the naked with clothing; if he not exacted usury nor taken any increase, but has withdrawn his hand from iniquity and executed true judgment between man and man. If he has walked in My statutes and kept My judgments faithfully; he is just; he shall surely live; says the Lord God (Ezekiel 18:5-9).

The soul who sins shall die. The son shall not bear the guilt of the father, nor the father bear the guilt of the son. The righteousness of the righteous shall be upon himself. But if a wicked man turns from all his sins which he has committed, keeps all my statutes and does what is lawful and right, he shall surely live; he shall not die. None of the transgressions which he has committed shall be remembered against him; because of the righteousness which he has done, he shall live (Ezekiel 18:20-22).

Do I have any pleasure at all that wicked should die? Says the Lord God, and not that he should turn from his ways and live (Ezekiel 18:23).

Now to Him who is able to keep you from stumbling, and to present you faultless before the presence of His glory with exceeding joy, to God our Savior, Who alone is wise, be glory and majesty, dominion and power, both now and forever (Jude 1:24-25).

Trust in the Lord with all your heart, and lean not on your own understanding; in all your ways acknowledge Him, and He shall direct your paths (Proverbs 3:5-6).

Do not be wise in your own eyes; fear the Lord and depart from evil. It will be health to your flesh and strength to your bones (Proverbs 3:7-8).

Take heed what you hear. With the same measure you use, it will be measured to you; and to you who hear, more will be given (Mark 4:24).

Whoever comes to Me, and hears My sayings and does them, I

will show you whom he is like:He is like a man building a house, who dug deep and laid the foundation on a rock. And when the flood arose, the stream beat vehemently against that house, and could not shake it, for it was founded on the rock (Luke 6:47-48).

And I say to you, My friends, do not be afraid of those who kill the body, and after that have no more that they can do. But I will show you whom you should fear: Fear Him who, after he has killed, has power to cast into hell; yes, I say to you, fear Him (Luke 12:4-5)!

But take heed to yourselves, lest your hearts be weighed down with carousing, drunkenness, and cares of this life, and that Day come on you unexpectedly. For it will come as a snare on all those who dwell on the face of the whole earth. Watch therefore; and pray always that you may be counted worthy to escape all these things that will come to pass, and to stand before the Son of Man (Luke 21:34-36).

John 4:24 states that, "God is a Spirit, and those who worship Him must worship in spirit and truth".

The thief does not come except to steal, and kill, and to destroy. I have come that they may have life, and that they may have it more abundantly (John 10:10).

There is no truth or mercy or knowledge of God in the land. By swearing and lying, killing and committing adultery, they break all restraint, with bloodshed upon bloodshed. Therefore, the land will mourn (Hosea 4:1-3).

My people are destroyed for lack of knowledge. Because you have rejected knowledge, I also will reject you from being priest for Me; because you have forgotten the law of your God, I will also forget your children (Hosea 4:6).

So I will punish them for their ways, and reward them for their deeds. For they shall eat, but not have enough; they shall eat, but not have enough; they shall commit harlotry, but not increase, because they have ceased obeying the Lord (Hosea 4:9-10).

Let us pursue the knowledge of the Lord. His going forth is established as the morning; He will come to us like the rain, like the latter and former rain to the earth (Hosea 6:3).

Come, and let us return to the Lord; for He has torn, but He will heal us; He has stricken, but He will bind us up (Hosea 6:1).

The Heart of God (Chapter 4)

Trust in the Lord, and do good; dwell in the land, and feed on His faithfulness. Delight yourself also in the Lord, and He shall give you the desires of your heart (Psalm 37:3).

Have faith in God. For assuredly, I say to you, whoever says to this mountain, Be removed and be cast into the sea, and does not doubt in his heart, but believes that those things he says will be done, he will have whatever he says (Mark 11:22-23).

Therefore I say to you, whatever things you ask when you pray, believe that you receive them, and you will have them (Mark 11:24).

Show me Your ways, O Lord; teach me Your paths. Lead me in your truth and teach me, for You are the God of my salvation; On You I wait all the day (Psalm 25:4).

Every good gift and every perfect gift is from above, and comes down from the Father of lights, with whom there is no variation or shadow of turning (James 1:17).

In this is love, not that we loved God, but that He loved us and sent His Son to be the propitiation for our sins (1 John 4:10).

Be anxious for nothing, but in everything by prayer and

supplication, with thanksgiving, let your requests be made known to God; and the peace of God, which surpasses all understanding, will guard your hearts and minds through Jesus (Philippians 4:6-7).

And my God shall supply all your need according to His riches in glory by Christ Jesus (Philippians 4:19).

Paul admonishes that we should always give "thanks to the Father who has qualified us to be partakers of the inheritance of the saints in the light. He has delivered us from the power of darkness and conveyed us into the kingdom of the Son of His love (Colossians 1:12-13).

1 Corinthians 2:9 states that "eye has not seen, nor ear heard, nor have it entered into the heart of man the things which God has prepared for those who love Him".

I say then, have they stumbled that they should fall? Certainly not! But through their fall, to provoke them to jealousy, salvation has come to the Gentiles (Romans 11:11).

And we know that all things work together for good to those who love God, to those who are the called according to His purpose (Romans 8:28).

Let no one say when he is tempted, "I am tempted by God"; for God cannot be tempted by evil, nor does He Himself tempt anyone. But each one is tempted when he is drawn away by his own desires and enticed (James 1:13-14).

But God, who is rich in mercy, because of His great love with which He loved us, even when we were dead in trespasses, made us alive together with Christ (by grace you have been saved), and raised us up together, and made us sit together in the heavenly places in Christ Jesus, that in the ages to come He might show the exceeding riches of His grace in His kindness toward us in Christ Jesus (Ephesians 2:4-7).

That He would grant you, according to the riches of His glory, to be strengthened with might through His Spirit in the inner man, that Christ may dwell in your hearts through faith; that you, being rooted and grounded in love, may be able to comprehend with all the saints what is the width and length and depth and height: to know the love of Christ which passes knowledge; that you may be filled with all the fullness of God (Ephesians 3:16-19).

Hebrews 6:14 states, "Surely blessing I will bless you, and multiplying I will multiply you". God swore by Himself when He made this promise to Abraham to show the immutability of His word and we are heir to this very promise as long as we believe and accept the salvation of our Lord and Savior Jesus Christ.

Thus God, determining to show more abundantly to the heirs of promise the immutability of His counsel confirmed it by oath, that by two immutable things, in which it is impossible for God to lie, we might have strong consolation, who have fled for refuge to lay hold of the hope set before us (Hebrews 6:17-18).

I, even I am He who comforts you. Who are you that you should be afraid of a man who will die, and of the son of man who will be made like grass? And forget the Lord your Maker, Who stretched out the heavens and laid the foundations of earth (Isaiah 51- 12-13).

But I am the Lord your God, And I have put My words in your mouth; I have covered you with the shadow of My hand (Isaiah 51:15-16).

Daniel 3:29, gives an account of how king Nebuchadnezzar decreed that anyone who spoke against the God of Shadrach, Meshach, and Abednego would be destroyed because "there is no other God who can deliver like this".

In Psalm 24:1 David declares that "the earth is the Lord's and all it's fullness, the world and those who dwell therein".

Scripture References

And whatever things you ask in prayer, believing, you will receive (Matthew 21:22).

When Jesus heard it, He departed from there by boat to a deserted place by Himself (Matthew 14:13).

Now it came to pass in those days that He went out to the mountain to pray, and continued all night in prayer to God (Luke 6:12).

And when He had sent the multitudes away, He went up on the mountain by Himself to pray. Now when evening came, He was alone there (Matthew 14:23).

But Jesus went to the Mount of Olives. Now early in the morning He came again into the temple, and all the people came to Him; and He sat down and taught them (John 8:1-2).

Behold, I give you the authority to trample on serpents and scorpions, and over all the power of the enemy, and nothing shall by any means hurt you (Luke 10:19).

Now in the morning, having risen a long while before daylight, He went out and departed to a solitary place; and there He prayed (Mark 1:35).

But when the Helper comes, whom I shall send to you from the Father, the Spirit of truth who proceeds from the Father, He will testify of Me (John 15:26).

For in Him we live and move and have our being, as also some of your own poets have said, for we are also His offspring (Acts 17:28).

The earth is the Lord's and all its fullness, the world and those that dwell therein (Psalm 24:1).

So we boldly say: "The Lord is my helper; I will not fear. What can man do to me" (Hebrews 13:6).

TRUSTING IN GOD

Come unto Me all ye that labor and are heavy laden and I will give you rest. Take My yoke upon you and learn from Me; For I am gentle and lowly of heart, and you will find rest for your souls. For My yoke is easy and My burden is light (Matthew 11:28-30).

These things I have spoken to you, that in Me you may have peace. In the world you will have tribulation; but be of good cheer, I have overcome the world (John 16:33).

And in that day you will ask Me nothing, Most assuredly, I say to you, whatever you ask the Father in My name He will give you. Until now you have asked nothing in My name. Ask, and you will receive, that your joy may be full (John 16:23-24).

Let not your heart be troubled; you believe in God, believe also in Me (John 14:1).

My sheep hear My voice, and I know them, and they follow Me. And I give them eternal life, and they shall never perish; neither shall anyone snatch them out of My hand. My Father, who has given them to Me, is greater than all; and no one is able to snatch them out of My Father's hand (John 10:27-29).

And which of you by worrying can add one cubit to his stature (Luke 12:25).

And do not seek what you should eat or what you should drink, nor have an anxious mind. For all these things the nations of the world seek after, and your Father knows that you need these things. But seek the kingdom of God, and all these things shall be added to you. Do not fear, little flock for it is you the kingdom (Luke 12:29-32).

But when you hear of wars and rumors of wars, do not be

troubled; for such things must happen, but the end is not yet (Mark 13:7).

Assuredly, I say to you, there is no one who has left house or brothers or sisters or father or mother or wife or children or lands, for My sake and the gospel's, who shall not receive a hundredfold now in this time; houses and brothers and sisters and mothers and children and lands, with persecutions – and in the age to come, eternal life (Mark 10:29-30).

However, when He, the Spirit of truth, has come, He will guide you into all truth; for He will not speak on His own authority, but whatever He hears He will speak; and He will tell you things to come (16:13).

But you are not willing to come to Me that you may have life. I do not receive honor from men (John 5:40-41).

Keep sound wisdom and discretion; so they will be life to your soul and grace to your neck. Then you will walk safely in your way, and your foot will not stumble. When you lie down, you will not be afraid; Yes you will lie down and your sleep will be sweet (Proverbs 3:21-24).

He who dwells in the secret place of the Most High shall abide under the shadow of the Almighty. I will say of the Lord, He is my refuge and my fortress; My God, in Him I will trust (Psalm 91:1-2).

A thousand may fall at your side, and ten thousand at your right hand; but it shall not come near you. Only with your eyes shall you look, and see the reward of the wicked (Psalm 91:7-8).

Because you have made the Lord, who is my refuge, even the Most High, your dwelling place, no evil shall befall you, nor shall any plague come near your dwelling; For He shall give His angels charge over you, to keep you in all your ways (Psalm 91:9-11).

Because he has set his love upon Me, therefore I will deliver him; I will set him on high, because he has known My name. He shall call upon Me, and I will answer him; I will be with him in trouble; I will deliver him and honor him. With long life I will satisfy him, and show him My salvation (Psalm 91:14-16).

All your children shall be taught by the Lord, and great shall be the peace of your children. In righteousness you shall be established: you shall be far from oppression, for you shall not fear; and from terror, for it shall not come near you (Isaiah 54:13-14).

Indeed they shall assemble, but not because of Me. Whoever assembles against you shall fall for you sake. No weapon formed against you shall prosper, and every tongue which rises against you in judgment you shall condemn. This is the heritage of the servants of the Lord, and their righteousness is from Me, says the Lord (Isaiah 54:15& 17).

And My elect shall long enjoy the work of their hands. They shall not labor in vain, nor bring forth children for trouble; for they shall be the descendants of the blessed of the Lord, and their offspring with them (Isaiah 65:23).

It shall come to pass that before they call, I will answer; and while they are still speaking, I will hear (Isaiah 65:24).

And do not be conformed to this world, but be transformed by the renewing of your mind, that you may prove what is that good and acceptable and perfect will of God (Romans 12:2).

This I say, therefore, and testify in the Lord, that you should no longer walk as the rest of the Gentiles walk, in the futility of their mind, having their understanding darkened, being alienated from the life of God, because of the blindness of their heart (Ephesians 4:17-18).

Having disarmed principalities and powers, He made a public

spectacle of them, triumphing over them in it (Colossians 2:15).

And you, being dead in your trespasses and the uncircumcision of your flesh, He has made alive together with Him, having forgiven you all trespasses having wiped out the handwriting of requirements that was against us, which was contrary to us. And He has taken it out of the way having nailed it to the cross (Colossians 2:13-14).

I will call them My people, who were not My people, and her beloved, who was not beloved. And it shall come to pass in the place where it said to them, you are My people, there they shall be called sons of the living God (Romans 9:25-26).

Fear not, for I have redeemed you; I have called you by your name; you are Mine. When you pass through the waters, I will be with you; and through the rivers, they shall not overflow you. When you walk through the fire, you shall not be burned, nor shall the flame scorch you (Isaiah 43:1-2).

I have been young, and now I am old; yet I have not seen the righteous forsaken, nor his descendants begging bread (Psalm 37:25).

But the salvation of the righteous is from the Lord; He is their strength in the time of trouble. And the Lord shall help them and deliver them; He shall deliver them from the wicked, and save them, because they trust in Him (Psalm 37:39-40).

Therefore the law was our tutor to bring us to Christ, that we might be justified by faith. But after faith has come, we are no longer under a tutor. For you are all sons of God through faith in Christ Jesus (Galatians 3:24-26).

Even the captives of the mighty shall be taken away, and the prey of the terrible be delivered; for I will contend with him who contends with you, and I will save your children. All flesh shall know that I, the Lord, am your Savior, and your Redeemer, the Mighty One of Jacob (49:25-26).

I, even I, am He who blots out your transgressions for My own sake; and I will not remember your sins, Put Me in remembrance; let us contend together; state your case, that you may be acquitted (Isaiah 43:25-26).

For since the beginning of the world Men have not heard nor perceived by ear, nor has the eye seen any God besides You, who acts for those who waits for Him. You meet him who rejoices and does righteousness, who remembers You in Your ways (Isaiah 64:4-5).

Truly, these times of ignorance God overlooked, but now commands all men everywhere to repent, because He has appointed a day on which He will judge the world in righteousness by the Man whom He has ordained. He has given assurance of this to all by raising Him from the dead (Acts 17:30-31).

THE ERROR OF OUR WAYS (CHAPTER 5)

You are of your father the devil, and the desires of your father you want to do. He was a murderer from the beginning, and does not stand in the truth, because there is no truth in him. When he speaks a lie, he speaks from his own resources, for he is a liar and the father of it (John 8:42).

For they loved the praise of men more than the praise of God (John 12:43).

How can you believe, who receive honor from one another and do not seek the honor that comes from the only God (John 5:44).

You are those who justify yourselves before men, but God knows your hearts. For what is highly esteemed among men is an abomination in the sight of God (Luke 16:15).

Scripture References

Why do you transgress the commandment of God because of your tradition? (Matthew 15:3).

These people draw near to Me with their mouth, and honor Me with their lips, and in vain they worship Me, teaching as doctrines the commandments of men (Matthew 15:8-9).

And because lawlessness will abound, the love of many will grow cold (Matthew 24:12).

There is nothing that enters a man from outside which can defile him; but the things which come out of him, those are things that defile a man (Mark 7:15)

My people are bent on backsliding from Me. Though they call to the Most High, none at all exalt Him (Hosea 11:7).

But everyone who hears these sayings of Mine and does not do them, will be like a foolish man who built his house on the sand: and the rain descended, the floods came, and the winds blew and beat on that house; and it fell. And great was that fall (Matthew 7:26-27).

For from within, out of the heart of men, proceed evil thoughts, adulteries, fornication, murders, thefts, covetousness, wickedness, deceit, lewdness, an evil eye, blasphemy, pride, foolishness. All these things come from within and defile a man (Mark 7:22-23).

Children how hard it is for those who trust in riches to enter the kingdom of God (Mark 10:24)!

Give to everyone who asks of you. And from him who takes away your goods do not ask them back. And just as you want men to do to you, you also do to them likewise. But if you love those who love you, what credit is that to you? For even sinners love those who love them (Luke 6:30-32).

Therefore, whatever you want men to do to you, do also to them, for this is the Law and the Prophets (Matthew 7:12).

Because narrow is the gate and difficult is the way which leads to life, and there are few who find it (Matthew 7:14).

Not everyone who says to Me Lord, Lord, shall enter the kingdom of heaven, but he who does the will of My Father in heaven. Many will say to Me in that day, Lord, Lord have we not prophesied in Your name, cast out demons in Your name, and done many wonders in Your name? And then I will declare to them, I never knew you; depart from Me, you who practice lawlessness (Matthew 7:21-23).

But love your enemies, do good, and lend, hoping for nothing in return; and your reward will be great, and you will be sons of the Most High. For He is kind to the unthankful and evil (Luke 6:35).

Therefore take heed that the light which is in you is not darkness (Luke 11:35).

Take heed and beware of covetousness for one's life does not consist in the abundance of the things he possesses (Luke 12:15).

And this is eternal life, that they may know You, the only true God, and Jesus Christ whom you have sent (John 17:3).

And they will fight against you, but they shall not prevail against you; for I am with you to save you and deliver you, says the Lord. I will deliver you from the hand of wicked, and I will redeem you from the grip of the terrible (Jeremiah 15:20-21).

Cursed is the man who trusts in man and makes flesh his strength, whose heart departs from the Lord. For he shall be like a shrub in the desert, and shall not see when good comes, but shall inhabit the parched places in the wilderness, in salt land which is not inhabited (17:5-6).

And you, who once were alienated and enemies in your mind

by wicked works, yet now He has reconciled in the body of His flesh through death, to present you holy, blameless, and above reproach in His sight; if indeed you continue in the faith grounded and steadfast, and are not moved away from the hope of the gospel which you heard, which was preached to every creature under heaven, of which I, Paul, became a minister (Colossians 1:21-13).

Because you have relied on the king of Syria, and have not relied on the Lord your God, therefore the army of the king of Syria has escaped from your hand (2 Chronicles 16:7).

For the eyes of the Lord run to and fro throughout the whole earth, to show Himself strong on behalf of those whose heart is loyal to Him. In this you have done foolishly; therefore from now on you shall have wars (2 Chronicles 16:9).

And in the thirty-ninth year of his reign, Asa became diseased in his feet, and his malady was severe; yet in his disease he did not seek the Lord, but the physicians (2 Chronicles 16:12).

And for this reason God will send them strong delusion, that they should believe the lie, that they all may be condemned who did not believe the truth but had pleasure in unrighteousness (2 Thessalonians 2:11-12).

But know this, that in the last days perilous times will come: for men will be lovers of themselves, lovers of money, boasters, proud, blasphemers, disobedient to parents, unthankful, unholy, unloving, unforgiving, slanderers, without self-control, brutal, despisers of good, traitors, headstrong, haughty, lovers of pleasure rather than lovers of God, having a form of godliness but denying its power. And from such people turn away (2 Timothy 3:1-5).

Whoever transgresses and does not abide in the doctrine in Christ does not have God. He who abides in the doctrine for Christ has both the Father and Son (2 John 1:9).

Do not be deceived: Evil company corrupts good habits (1 Corinthians 15:33).

Do you know that all the saints will judge the world? And if the world will be judged by you, are you unworthy too judge the smallest matters? (1 Corinthians 6:2).

I wrote to you in my epistle not to keep company with sexually immoral people. Yet I certainly did not mean with the sexually immoral people of this world, or with the covetous, or extortioners, or idolaters, since then you would need to go out of the world (1 Corinthians 5:9-10)

If your enemy is hungry, feed him; if he is thirsty, give him a drink; for in so doing you will heap coals of fire on his head. Do not be overcome by evil, but overcome evil with good (Romans 12:20-21).

For they being ignorant of God's righteousness, and seeking to establish their own righteousness, have not submitted to the righteousness of God (Romans 10:3).

But avoid foolish disputes, genealogies, contentions, and strivings about the law; for they are unprofitable and useless (Titus 3:9).

For sin shall not have dominion over you, for you are not under law but under grace (Romans 6:14).

However, the Most High does not dwell in temples made with hands, as the prophet says: Heaven is My throne, and earth is My footstool, what house will you build for Me says the Lord, or what is the place of My rest? Has My hand not made all these things? (Acts 7:48-50).

What purpose then does the law serve? It was added because of transgressions, till the Seed should come to whom the promise was made; and it was appointed through angels by the hand of a mediator (Galatians 3:19).

Scripture References

If indeed you have heard Him and have been taught by Him, as the truth is in Jesus: that you put off, concerning your former conduct, the old man which grows corrupt according to deceitful lusts, and be renewed in the spirit of your mind, and that you put on the new man which was created according to God, in true righteousness and holiness (Ephesians 4:21-24).

Finally, brethren, whatever things are true, whatever things are noble, whatever things are just, whatever things are pure, whatever things are lovely, whatever, things are of good report, if there be any virtue and if there is anything praiseworthy: meditate on these things (Philippians 4:8).

Inasmuch as these people draw near with their mouths and honor Me with their lips, but have removed their hearts far from Me, and their fear toward Me is taught by the commandments of men (Isaiah 29:13).

For shall the thing made say of him who made it, He did not make me? Or shall the thing formed say of him who formed it, He has no understanding? (Isaiah 29:16)

My people have committed two evils: they have forsaken Me, the fountain of living waters, and hewn themselves cisterns; broken cisterns that can hold no water (Jeremiah 2:13).

Your own wickedness will correct you, and your backslidings will rebuke you. Know therefore and see that it is an evil and bitter thing that you have forsaken the Lord your God and the fear of Me is not in you, says the Lord God of Hosts (Jeremiah 2:19).

Blessed is the man who walks not in the counsel of the ungodly, nor stands in the path of sinners, nor sits in the seat of the scornful; but his delight is in the law of the Lord, and in His law he meditates day and night. He shall be like a tree planted by the rivers of water, that brings forth its fruit in its season, whose leaf also shall not wither; and whatever he does shall prosper (Psalms 1:1-3).

Know that the Lord He is God; it is He who made us, and not we ourselves; we are His people and sheep of His pasture (Psalm 100:3).

Kingdom Ambassadors

If I then, your Lord and Teacher, have washed your feet, you also ought to wash one another's feet (John 13:14).

If you know these things, blessed are you if you do them (John 13:17).

Most assuredly, I say to you, he who believes in Me, the works that I do he will do also; and greater works than these he will do, because I go to My Father. And whatever you ask in My name, that I will do, that the Father may be glorified in the Son. If you ask anything in My name, I will do it (John 14:12-14).

If you love Me, keep My commandments. If anyone loves Me, he will keep My word; and My Father will love him, and we will come to him and make Our home with him (John 14:15 & 23).

But the Helper, the Holy Spirit, whom the Father will send in My name, He will teach you all things, and bring to your remembrance all things that I said to you. Peace I leave with you, My peace I give to you; not as the world gives do I give to you. Let not your heart be troubled, neither let it be afraid (John 14:26-27).

If you abide in Me and My words abide in you, you will ask what you desire, and it shall be done for you. By this My Father is glorified, that you bear much fruit; so you will be My disciples (John 15:7-8).

But if I cast out demons by the Spirit of God, surely the kingdom of heaven has come upon you (Matthew 12-28).

Scripture References

But whoever causes one of these little one to stumble, it would be better for Him if a millstone were hung around his neck, and he were thrown into the sea (Mark 9:42).

Yet it shall not be so among you: but whoever desires to become great among you shall be servant. And whoever of you desires to be first shall be slave of all. For even the Son of Man did not come to be served, but to serve, and to give His life a ransom for many (Mark 10:43-45).

And these signs will follow those who believe: In My name they will cast out demons; they will speak with new tongues; they will take up serpents; and if they drink anything deadly, it will by no means hurt them; they will lay hands on the sick and they will recover (Mark 16:17-18).

My kingdom is not of this world. If My kingdom were of this world, My servants would fight, so that I should not be delivered to the Jews; but now My kingdom is not from here (John 18:36).

Give and it will be given to you: good measure, pressed down, shaken together, and running over will be put into your bosom. For with the same measure that you use, it will be measured back to you (Luke 6:38).

And as you go, preach, saying the kingdom of heaven is at hand. Heal the sick, cleanse the lepers, raise the dead, cast out demons. Freely you have received, freely give (Matthew 10:7-8).

But he who did not know, yet committed things deserving of stripes, shall be beaten with few. For everyone to whom much is given, from him much will be required; and to whom much has been committed, of him they will ask the more (Luke 12:48).

The kingdom of heaven does not come with observation; nor will they say, 'See here!' or 'See there!' For indeed, the kingdom of God is within you (Luke 17:21).

Let the little children come to Me, and do not forbid them; for such is the kingdom of God. Assuredly, I say to you, whoever does not receive the kingdom of God as a little child will by no means enter it (Luke 18:16-17).

Therefore thus says the Lord God; "Behold My servants shall eat, but you shall be hungry; Behold My servants shall drink, but you shall be thirsty; Behold My servants shall rejoice, But you shall be ashamed; Behold My servants shall sing for joy of heart, But you shall cry for sorrow of heart and wail for grief of spirit (Isaiah 65:13-14).

My elect shall long enjoy the work of their hands. They shall not labor in vain, nor bring forth children for trouble; for they shall be the descendants of the blessed of the Lord, and their offspring with them. It shall come to pass that before they call, I will answer; and while they are still speaking, I will hear (Isaiah 65:22-24).

Rejoice in the Lord your God; for He has given you the former rain faithfully, and He will cause the rain to come down for you: the former rain and the latter rain in the first month. The threshing floors shall be full of wheat, and the vats shall overflow with new wine and oil (Joel 2:23-24).

You shall eat in plenty and be satisfied, and praise the name of the Lord your God, who has dealt wondrously with you; and My people shall never be put to shame (Joel 2:26).

Therefore, behold, I will again do a marvelous work among this people, a marvelous work and a wonder; for the wisdom of the wise men shall perish, and the understanding of their prudent men shall be hidden (Isaiah 29:14).

God anointed Jesus of Nazareth with the Holy Spirit and with power, who went about doing good and healing all who were oppressed by the devil, for God was with Him (Acts 10:38).

Scripture References

And we desire that each one of you show the same diligence to the full assurance of hope until the end; that you do not become sluggish, but imitate those who through faith and patience inherit the promises (Hebrews 6:11-12).

Is anyone among you suffering? Let him sing psalms. Is anyone among you sick? Let him call for the elders of the church, and let them pray over him, anointing him with oil in the name of the Lord. And the prayer of faith will save the sick, and the Lord will raise him up. And if he has committed sins he will be forgiven (James 5:13-15).

Therefore gird up the loins of your mind, be sober, and rest your hope fully upon the grace that is to be bought to you at the revelation of Jesus Christ; as obedient children, not conforming yourselves to the former lusts, as in your ignorance; but as He who called you is holy, you also be holy in all your conduct, because it is written, Be holy for I am holy (1 Peter 1:13-16).

For you are the temple of the living God. As God has said: I will dwell in them and walk among them. I will be their God, and they shall be My people (2 Corinthians 6:16).

Now the Lord is a Spirit; and where the Spirit of the Lord is there is liberty (2 Corinthians 3:17).

Therefore, do not let your good be spoken of as evil: For the kingdom of God is not eating and drinking, but righteousness and peace and joy in the Holy Spirit (Romans 14:16-17).

Repay no one evil for evil. Have regard for good things in the sight of all men. If it is possible, as much as depends on you, live peaceably with all men (Romans 12:17-18).

Now God worked unusual miracles by the hands of Paul, so that even handkerchiefs or aprons were brought from his body to the sick, and the diseases left them and the evil spirits went out of them (Acts 19:11).

But you are a chosen generation, a royal priesthood, a holy nation, His own special people, that you may proclaim the praises of Him who called you out of darkness into His marvelous light; who once were not a people but are now the people of God, who had not obtained mercy but now obtained mercy (1 Peter 2:9-10).

This book of the Law shall not depart from your mouth, but you shall meditate in it day and night, that you may observe to do according to all that is written in it. For then you will make your way prosperous, and then you will have good success (Joshua 1:8).

Death and life are in the power of the tongue, and those who love it will eat its fruit (Proverbs 18:21).

Walk worthy of the calling with which you were called, with all lowliness and gentleness, with longsuffering, bearing with one another in love, endeavoring to keep the unity of the Spirit in the bond of peace (Ephesians 4:1-3).

Then it shall come to pass, because you listen to these judgments, and keep and do them, that the Lord your God will keep with you the covenant and the mercy which He swore to your fathers. He will love you and bless you and multiply you. You shall be blessed above all peoples. And the Lord will take away from you all sickness (Deuteronomy 7:12-15).

But I make known to you brethren, that the gospel which was preached by me is not according to man. For I neither received it from man, nor was taught it, but it came through the revelation of Jesus Christ (Galatians 1:11-12).

Therefore, as elect of God, holy and beloved, put on tender mercies, kindness, humility, meekness, longsuffering; bearing with one another, and forgiving one another, if anyone has a complaint against another; even as Christ forgave you, so you also must do. But above all things out on love, which is the bond of perfection. And let the peace of God rule in your hearts, to which also you were called in one body; and be thankful (Colossians 3:12-14).

Preach the word! Be ready in season and out of season and out of season. Convince, rebuke, exhort, with all longsuffering and teaching. For the time will come when they will not endure sound doctrine, but according to their own desires, because they have itching ears, they will heap up for themselves teachers; and they will turn their ears away from the truth, and be turned aside fables (2 Timothy 4:2-4).

And let your people also learn to maintain good works, to meet urgent needs, that they may not be unfruitful (Titus (3:14).

But the end of all things is at hand; therefore be serious and watchful in your prayers. And above all things have fervent love for one another, for love will cover a multitude of sins (1 Peter 4:7-8).

Repent, and turn from all your transgressions, so that iniquity will not be your ruin. Cast away from you all the transgressions which you have committed, and get yourselves a new spirit. For why should you die, O house of Israel? For I have no pleasure in the death of one who dies, says the Lord God. Therefore turn and live (Ezekiel 18:30-32).

Let your light so shine before men, that they may see your good works and glorify your Father in heaven (Matthew 5:16).

PRINCIPLES & PRECEPTS FOR MEN AND WOMEN OF GOD (CHAPTERS 6 AND 7)

Have you not read that He made them at the beginning made them male and female, and said For this reason a man shall leave his father and mother and joined to his wife, and the two shall become one flesh (Matthew 19:4-5).

This is My commandment that you love one another as I have loved you (John 15:12).

Blessed are the merciful, for they shall obtain mercy (Matthew 5:7).

Oh the depth of the riches both of the wisdom and knowledge of God! How unsearchable are His judgments and His ways past finding out (Romans 11:33).

All scripture is given by inspiration of God, and is profitable for doctrine, for reproof, for correction, for instruction in righteousness, that the man of God may be complete, thoroughly equipped for every good work (2 Timothy 3:16-17).

I desire therefore that the men pray everywhere, lifting up holy hands, without wrath and doubting (1 Timothy 2:8).

Likewise, exhort the young men to be sober-minded, in all things showing yourself to be a pattern of good works; in doctrine showing integrity, reverence, incorruptibility (Titus 2:6-7).

Husbands, likewise, dwell with them with understanding, giving honor to the wife, as to the weaker vessel, and as being heirs together of the grace of life, that your prayers may not be hindered (1 Peter 3:7).

Be sober, be vigilant, because your adversary the devil walks about like a roaring lion, seeking whom he may devour (1 Peter 5:8).

Husbands, love your wives, just as Christ also loved the church and gave Himself for her. So husbands ought to love their own wives as their own bodies; he who loves his wife loves himself: For no one ever hated his own flesh, but nourishes and cherishes it, just as the Lord does the church (Ephesians 5:25, 28-29).

Scripture References

Let deacons be husbands of one wife, ruling their children and their own houses well. For those who have served well as deacons obtain for themselves a good standing and great boldness in the faith which is Christ Jesus (1 Timothy 3:12-13).

A new commandment I give to you, that you love one another; as I have loved you, that you also love one another. By this all will know that you are My disciples, if you have love for one another (John 13:34-35).

Blessed are the meek, for they shall inherit the earth (Matthew 5:5).

Whatever your hand finds to do, do it with all your might; for there is no work or device or knowledge or wisdom in the grave where you are going (Ecclesiastes 9:10).

Submitting to one another in the fear of God. Wives, submit to your own husbands, as to the Lord. For the husband is the head of the wife, as also Christ is head of the church; and He is the Savior of the body. Therefore, just as the church is subject to Christ, so let wives be to their own husbands in everything (Ephesians 5:21-24).

Does the potter have power over the clay, from the same lump to make one vessel for honor and another for dishonor? (Romans 9:21).

And on the Sabbath day we went out of the city to the riverside, where prayer was customarily made; and we sat down and spoke to the women who met there (Acts 16:13).

For it is God who works in you both to will and to do for His good pleasure. Do all things without complaining and disputing (Philippians 2:13-14).

In like manner also, that the women adorn themselves in modest apparel, with propriety and moderation, not with braided hair or gold or pearls or costly clothing, but which is proper for women professing godliness, with good works (1 Timothy 2:9-10).

Let a woman learn in silence with all submission. And I do not permit a woman to teach or have authority over a man, but to be in silence (1 Timothy 2:11-12).

Know the Lord, He is God; it He who has made us, and not we ourselves; we are His people and the sheep of His pasture (Psalm 100:3).

And they said, "That is hopeless! So we will walk according to our own plans, and we will every one obey the dictates of his evil heart (Jeremiah 18:12).

But when you thus sin against the brethren, and wound their weak conscience, you sin against Christ. Therefore, if food makes my brother stumble, I will never again eat meat, lest I make my brother stumble (1 Corinthians 8:12-13).

The older women likewise, that they be reverent in behavior, not slanderers, not given to much wine, teachers of good things: that they admonish the young women to love their husbands, to love their children, to be discreet, chaste, homemakers, good, obedient to their own husbands, that the word of God many not be blasphemed (Titus 2:3-5).

The Most High God rules in the kingdom of men, and appoints over it whomever He chooses (Daniel 5:21).

Humble yourselves in the sight of the Lord, and He will lift you up (James 4:10).

Wives, likewise, be submissive to your own husbands, that even if some do not obey the word, they without a word, may be won by the conduct of their wives, when they observe your chaste conduct accompanied by fear. Do not let your adornment be merely outward: arranging the hair, wearing the gold, or putting on fine apparel. Rather let it be the hidden person of the heart, with the incorruptible beauty of a gentle and quiet spirit, which is very precious in the sight of God (1 Peter 3:1-4).

For in this manner, in former times, the holy women who trusted in God also adorned themselves being submissive to their own husbands, as Sarah obeyed Abraham calling him lord, whose daughters you are if you do good and are not afraid of any terror (1 Peter 3:5-6).

He who finds a wife finds a good thing, and obtains favor from the Lord (Proverbs 18:22).

Charm is deceitful and beauty is passing, but a woman who fears the Lord, she shall be praised (Proverbs 31:30).

I will greatly multiply your sorrow and conception; in pain you shall bring forth children; your desire shall be for your husband, and he shall rule over you (Genesis 3:16).

In sweat of your face you shall eat bread till you return to the ground, for out of it you were taken; for dust you are and to dust you shall return (Genesis 3:19).

BASKING IN JESUS (CHAPTER 9)

Nevertheless I tell you the truth. It is to your advantage that I go away; for if I do not go away, the Helper will not come to you; but if I depart, I will send Him to you (John 16:7).

And He who sent Me is with Me. The Father has not left Me alone, for I always do those things that please Him (John 8:29).

If you abide in My word, you are My disciples indeed. And you shall know the truth, and the truth shall make you free (John 8:31-32).

I have come as a light into the world, that whoever believes in Me should not abide in darkness. And if anyone hears My words and does not believe, I do not judge him; for I did not come to judge the world but to save the world. He who rejects Me, and does not receive My words, has that which judges him: the word that I have spoken will judge him in the last day (John 12:46-48).

And I, if I am lifted up from the earth, will draw all peoples to Myself (John 12:32).

You do not know what manner of spirit you are of. For the Son of Man did not come to destroy men's lives but to save them (Luke 9:55-56).

And the word became flesh and dwelt among us, and we beheld His glory, the glory as of the only begotten of the Father, full of grace and truth (John 1:14).

For the law was given through Moses, but grace and truth came through Jesus Christ (John 1:17).

And a slave does not abide in the house forever, but a son abides forever. Therefore if the Son makes you free, you shall be free indeed (John 8:35-36).

I am the way, the truth and the life. No one comes to the Father except through Me (John 14:6).

I pray for them. I do not pray for the world but for those whom You have given Me, for they are Yours. And all mine are Yours, and Yours are mine, and I am glorified in them (John 17:9-10).

All that the Father gives Me will come to Me, and the one who comes to Me I will by no means cast out. And this is the will of Him who sent Me, that everyone who sees the Son and believes in Him may have everlasting life; and I will raise him up at the last day (John 6:37 & 40).

Scripture References

And they shall all be taught by God. Therefore, everyone who has heard and learned from the Father comes to Me (John 6:45).

It is the Spirit who gives life; the flesh profits nothing. The words that I speak to you are spirit, and they are life. Therefore I have said to you that no one can come to Me unless it has been granted to him by My Father (John 6:63 & 65).

And I will pray the Father, and He will give you another Helper, that He may abide with you forever: the Spirit of truth, whom the world cannot receive, because it neither sees Him nor knows Him; but you know Him, for He dwells with you and will be in you (John 14:16-17).

I am the light of the world. He who follows me shall not walk in darkness, but have the light of life (John 8:12).

Most assuredly, I say to you, I am the door of the sheep. All who ever came before Me are thieves and robbers, but the sheep did not hear them. I am the door. If anyone enters by Me, he will be saved, and will go in and out and find pasture (John 10:7-9).

The name of the Lord is a strong tower; the righteous run to it and are safe (Proverbs 18:10).

It has now been revealed by the Spirit of His holy apostles and prophets: that the Gentiles should be fellow heirs, of the same body, and partakers of His promise in Christ through the gospel (Ephesians 3:5-6).

To make all see what is the fellowship of the mystery [...] according to the eternal purpose which He accomplished in Christ our Lord, in whom we have boldness and access with confidence through faith in Him (Ephesians 3:9, 11-12).

Therefore God also has highly exalted Him and given Him the name which is above every name, that at the name of Jesus every knee should bow, of those in heaven, and of those on earth, and that every tongue should confess that Jesus Christ is Lord, to the glory of God the Father (Philippians 2:9-11).

I have suffered the loss of all things, and count them as rubbish, that I may gain Christ and be found in Him, not having my own righteousness, which is from the law, but that which is through faith in Christ, the righteousness which is from God by faith (Philippians 3:8-9).

For by Him all things were created that are in heaven and that are on earth, visible and invisible, whether thrones or dominions or principalities or powers. All things were created through Him and for Him (Colossians 1:16).

For it pleased the Father that in Him all the fullness should dwell, and by Him to reconcile all things to Himself, by Him, whether things on earth or things in heaven, having made peace through the blood of His cross (Colossians 1:19-20).

But thanks be to God, who gives us the victory through our Lord Jesus Christ (1 Corinthians 15:57).

Now He who searches the hearts knows what the mind of the Spirit is, because He makes intercession for the saints according to the will of God (Romans 8:27).

For as many as are led by the Spirit of God, these are sons of God. For you did not receive the spirit of bondage again to fear, but you received the Spirit of adoption by whom we cry out Abba Father (Romans 8:14-15).

The Spirit Himself bears witness with our spirit that we are children of God, and if children, then heirs: heirs of God and joint heirs with Christ, if indeed we suffer with Him, that we may also be glorified together (Romans 8:16-17).

For all have sinned and fall short of the glory of God, being justified freely by His grace through the redemption that is in

Scripture References

Christ Jesus (Romans 3:23-24).

Therefore let it be known to you, brethren, that through this Man is preached to you the forgiveness of sins; and by Him everyone who believes is justified from all things from which you could not be justified by the law of Moses (Acts 13:23-24).

Whoever believes that Jesus is the Christ is born of God, and everyone who loves Him who begot also loves him who is begotten of Him. By this we know that we love the children of God, when we love God and keep His commandments. For this is the love of God that keep we keep His commandments. And His commandments are not burdensome (1 John 5:1-3).

For whatever is born of God overcomes the world. And this is the victory that has overcome the world: our faith (1 John 3:4).

Therefore remember that you once were Gentiles in the flesh by hands: that at that time you were without Christ, being aliens from the commonwealth of Israel and strangers from the covenants of promise, having no hope and without God in the world. But now in Christ Jesus you who once were far off have been brought near by the blood of Christ (Ephesians 2:11-13).

Though He was a Son, yet He learned obedience by the things which He suffered. And having been perfected, He became the author of eternal salvation to all who obey Him (Hebrews 5:8-9).

I have set you as a light to the Gentiles, that you should be for salvation to the ends of the earth (Acts 13:47).

This is the stone which was rejected by you the builders, which has become the chief cornerstone. Nor is there salvation in any other, for there is no other name under heaven given among men by which we must be saved (Acts 4:11-12).

I have been crucified with Christ; it is no longer I who live, but Christ lives in me; and the life which I now live in flesh I live by faith in the Son of God, who loved me and gave Himself for me. I do not set aside the grace of God; for if righteousness comes through the law, then Christ died in vain (Galatians 2:20-21).

But when the fullness of the time had come, God sent forth His Son, born of a woman, born under law, to redeem those who were under the law, that we might receive the adoption as sons. And because you are sons, God has sent forth the Spirit of His Son into your hearts, crying out Abba Father (Galatians 4:4-6).

Stand fast therefore in the liberty by which Christ has made us free, and do not be entangled again with a yoke of bondage (Galatians 5:1).

For you, brethren, have been called to liberty; only do not use liberty as an opportunity for the flesh, but through love serve one another (Galatians 5:13).

Indeed He says, it is too small a thing that You should be My Servant to raise up the tribes of Jacob, and restore the preserved ones of Israel; I will also give You as a light to the Gentiles, that You should be My salvation to the ends of the earth (Isaiah 49:6).

I will preserve You and give You as a covenant to the people, to restore the earth, to cause them to inherit the desolate heritages; that You may say to the prisoners, go forth, to those who are in darkness, show yourselves (Isaiah 49:8-9).

Therefore take up the whole armor of God, that you may be able to withstand in the evil day, and having done all, to stand (Ephesians 6:13).

For until the law sin was in the world, but sin is not imputed when there is no law (Romans 5:13).

According to the grace of God which was given to me, as a wise master builder I have laid the foundation, and another builds on it. But let each one take heed how he builds on it. For no other foundation can anyone lay than that which is laid, which is Jesus Christ (1 Corinthians 3:10-11).

www.ingramcontent.com/pod-product-compliance
Lightning Source LLC
Chambersburg PA
CBHW031112080526
44587CB00011B/947